What Is the Gospel?

— It Is Finished

by John M. Drickamer

What Is the Gospel?

Copyright 1991 by John M. Drickamer.
All rights reserved. No part of this publication may be reproduced, stored in a retrieval system, or transmitted, in any form or by any means, electronic, mechanical, photocopying, recording, or otherwise, without the prior written permission of Lutheran News.

Lutheran News, Inc.
Manufactured in the
United States of America 2022
IngramSpark, TN
ISBN 978-1-7366844-7-4

ACKNOWLEDGMENTS

I wish to thank Pastor Herman Otten of Trinity Lutheran Church, New Haven, Missouri, who is the editor of *Christian News* (Lutheran News, Inc., 684 Luther Lane, New Haven, Missouri, 63068). These articles were all originally published in that weekly newspaper, and without that opportunity to publish them it is doubtful that many or any of them would have been written.

I also wish to thank Mr. Timothy Otten, the business manager of *Christian News,* who scanned all of these items into the computer and in other ways also assisted with their publication in this book form.

Finally, I wish to thank Mr. Charles Provan of Zimmer Printing for advice and assistance throughout the process of bringing this book to publication and for handling the business end of the whole matter.

Even with the help of all these people, I alone bear the responsibility for the contents of these pages, including any errors that may have crept in and not been located and corrected. If there is anything good in these pages, it has come only from God through His written word, the Bible. To God alone be glory!

Contents

What Is the Gospel 1
Constant Grace 4
The Gospel in Context 10
Law and Gospel 14
Sure Salvation 21
The Fear of the Lord 24
Jesus Is Lord! 26
Truly This Was the Son of God 28
On The Cross 32
Peace, Be Still! 36
Fears, Tears, and Years 38
The Long Haul 40
The Road to Capernaum 42
The Tiny Casket 44
A Tree Gave Its Life 45
Dimensions of Love 46
Acceptance and Forgiveness 48
Of Space and Salvation 50
Combined Parables 52
Power Versus Speed 55
God's Book 57
The Chosen Witnesses 59
The Importance of Theism 63
Specific Christianity 66
What Is God? 69
The Age Old New Age Movement 72
The Shepherd 75
He Must Increase 77
How Baptism Saves 79
Three Letters on Communion 83
How Are You? 89
Because We Love Them 92
Are We Proud? 96
Are We Aloof? 98

False Fellowship Is Unreal 101
Prayer Fellowship 105
Prayer and Faith 108
An Emphasis on Works 111
How to Love 113
God's Faithfulness 115
Whom Do You Trust? 117
How Shall They Believe? 119
Thank God, We Are Christians 121
How Do You Spell Faith? 123
The Unfree Will 125
What Is Truth? 128
The Human Heart 130
The Overall Theme 132
Summary 134
The Word of His Grace 137
Because I Live - An Easter Play 142

WHAT IS THE GOSPEL?

The Gospel is the good news about Jesus Christ and all that He has done for the salvation of sinners. The English word "Gospel" and the Greek word it translates both mean "good news." The Greek word is behind the words "evangelize," "evangelism," and "evangelical."

God the Father loved us sinners so much that He sent His Son to be our Savior (John 3:16). Jesus Christ is both God and Man. He lived the sinless life that we should have lived. But He became guilty in God's eyes for our sin. He died for our guilt. He completely suffered the punishment that we deserved. He earned the forgiveness of sins and eternal life for all mankind (John 1:29; 1 John 2:2). To prove that, He rose from the dead, coming back to life in His body (1 Corinthians 15).

The Gospel is good news. But we know it as good news only when we have first been convinced of the bad news (Romans 6:23). The bad news is the Law of God. There is nothing wrong with the Law. But there is plenty wrong with us. That Law is bad news because we are sinners. The Law would not condemn us if we were not sinners. The Law is the bad news of God's anger against sin.

A person who has heard the condemnation of the Law needs to hear the consolation of the Gospel. The Law is about God's anger because of sin. The Gospel is about God's grace because of Christ. Grace is the opposite of anger. God's grace is His favorable attitude toward sinners, in spite of their sin, because of their Savior.

The Gospel is unique. Only Christianity is the Gospel religion. Every other religion is the Law religion. Every other religion teaches self-salvation. Christianity is the religion of salvation by God. Every other religion teaches that our works can lead to salvation. Christianity teaches that our works can only lead to damnation. Every other religion tells us to try to go up to heaven. Christianity tells us that God came down to us to lift us up to heaven.

Every other religion is a do-it-yourself religion. Christianity is the done-for-you-by-Christ religion. Every other religion teaches that salvation results *from* good works. Christianity teaches that salvation results *in* good works (1 John 4:9). Every other religion boils down to some theory about God plus some do's and don'ts. Christianity emphasizes the word <u>done</u>, what Christ has accomplished for us.

Every other religion is a religion of faith in man and his works. Christianity is the religion of faith in God and His works. Only Christianity should be called a faith. Every other religion is a religion of earning and achieving. Christianity is the religion of receiving gifts from God, given although we have deserved only punishment. Every human religion is contrary to the Christian religion. Those who do not believe the Gospel are offended by it. They are proud of their own religious inventions and do not want to hear that Jesus is the only Savior (John 14:6).

But must a person not do one thing to be saved? Must he not believe the Gospel? A Christian does believe the Gospel. He trusts Jesus. But believing, trusting, having faith is not our work. Too many Christians want to spell faith with a capital I in the middle, emphasizing the believer. We should spell faith with a small i kneeling at the foot of the next letter, the cross, emphasizing Christ. The capital I in Christian spelling is in the word sin.

What is faith? Faith is belief and faith is trust. Faith is believing the facts of the Gospel: God the Son died for my sin and rose again from the dead; for His sake God has forgiven all my sins, so that I will not be damned to hell but welcomed into heaven forever. Faith is trusting God that this forgiveness is real because of Christ. There is no difference between faith as belief and faith as trust. Trusting a person to drive safely is the same as believing that he is a safe driver.

Christian faith is not a human achievement. It is a gift of God. We cannot choose to believe the Gospel, to have faith in Christ (John 6:29, 44; 1 Corinthians 2:14; 12:3). We do not choose to believe anything. We do not choose to believe that today's weather is bright and sunny. We believe that the day is sunny or rainy depending on what comes down from the sky and makes an impression on our eyes and skin.

We must be convinced from above that God is angry or gracious. The Law convinces us of God's anger against sin. The Gospel convinces us of God's grace and forgiveness for Jesus' sake. We trust a person because he has convinced us that he is trustworthy. We trust Christ because by His Word He has convinced us to trust Him. The seriousness of false doctrine is not in mistaken notions but in misplaced trust. Believing in a false god is not trusting the true God. Believing falsely about the true God is not trusting Him according to His Word and promise.

There is only one true God, the Triune God: Father, Son, and Holy Ghost. We are all sinful by nature and have all deserved by our sinfulness and by our many sinful thoughts, words, and deeds to be punished in hell forever. But God the Son took human nature upon Himself, becoming truly human. He kept the Law of God, which we have broken. He was crucified in our place, bearing the guilt and suffering the punishment for all our sins. He has appeased God's anger. Our sins have been forgiven. For Jesus' sake God has declared and pronounced us not guilty.

The faith that trusts and receives this forgiveness has been created and is preserved in us by the Holy Ghost, using the Word, Baptism, Absolution, and the Lord's Supper as His tools. Good works have nothing to do with getting us into heaven. That has been completely taken care of by Jesus. Then the Gospel, God's Word of grace and love, motivates and empowers us to begin to love God, Who has loved us first, and to love our neighbor, whom God has also loved. In this way we begin to do truly good, selfless, loving works.

The Triune God is the only true God. The Gospel of Jesus Christ is the only spiritual good news. Christianity is the only valid religion. "For all have sinned, and come short of the glory of God; being justified freely by His grace through the redemption that is in Christ Jesus" (Romans 3:23-24).

CONSTANT GRACE

Shakespeare's Hamlet was a legalist. He decided not to kill his uncle while the latter was at prayer. He thought that his uncle would go to heaven if he died then. He wanted his uncle to die at a time when he would go to hell.

That is the ingrained legalism of fallen men. We think that there must be requirements for us to meet to be saved. Legalism makes salvation an on-again-off-again proposition. We hope to die when we are meeting the requirements rather than when we are falling short.

But none of us ever draws a sinless breath in this world. Any thought of conditions for us to meet is impractical because it is impossible. Jesus has already satisfied the conditions for us and for all. That is the Gospel.

An amnesty is in effect because the king has decided to grant it. Then the news is spread. The news does not cause the amnesty. Believing the news does not cause the amnesty. Gratefully resolving to be a good citizen does not cause the amnesty. The king caused the amnesty by deciding to grant it.

The forgiveness of sins is in effect because God has accepted Christ's sacrifice on the cross for the sin of the world. Proclaiming it and believing it do not cause it. The proclaiming and the believing would be false if the forgiveness was not already in effect. It was in effect even before Christ died because God is not within time. It was as sure when promised as when fulfilled. So it was proclaimed and believed from Adam's time.

The Law says that we cannot meet any conditions. Christ has met all the conditions for us. But the old Adam still wants to claim some share of the credit and the glory. Before God's bar of justice, sinful men want to plead not guilty. Those who plead not guilty are convicted. *The surprise, offense, and joy of the Gospel is that we plead guilty and are acquitted for Jesus' sake.* We want to believe that we deserve to be acquitted. Like Little Jack Horner, we each want to say, "What a good boy am I!" That is Pharisaism, Romanism—any and every version of works righteousness. Most people believe some version of it. There but for the grace of God go you and I!

If Christ has met the conditions for all, why are not all saved? The Bible does not tell us that. We are to rest content without having that question answered to the satisfaction of proud human reason. The history of false doctrine is full of human attempts to answer it. The good news is that we are saved entirely apart from any works or worthiness of our own, entirely by Christ's righteousness, merit, blood, and sacrifice for us in our place.

God loves the world (John 3:16). He loves every person in the world. Christ died for all (2 Corinthians 5:15). He fully atoned for all the sins of every human sinner. Propitiation means rendering someone's attitude favorable. Jesus propitiated God, satisfied God's anger against our sin, and earned for us God's grace, God's favorable attitude. He did that for everyone (1 John 2:2). A person is converted or regenerated (born again) when God through the Gospel brings him to trust that his sins have been forgiven for Jesus' sake. That is faith in Christ.

A believer in Christ trusts that all his sins have been atoned for by Christ and forgiven by God (Colossians 2:13-14; Psalm 85:2-3; 103:3; Isaiah 38:17; 43:25; 2 Corinthians 5:19; 1 John 1:7; and many more). The forgiveness of all sin was caused, effected, brought about, produced, realized by Christ's sacrifice on the cross (John 19:30: "It is finished!"). It is announced, offered, bestowed, given, and assured by the Gospel in all its forms (including Absolution, Baptism, Communion). It is fully received by faith, which is worked, produced, strengthened, confirmed by the Holy Ghost through the Gospel in all its forms.

We have grace, forgiveness, life, and salvation because of Christ through faith, not through Christ because of faith. If it were because of faith, faith would save us as a good work. We would be back in works righteousness. But Christ has saved us. Faith receives the gift. It does not cause the gift. Christ has made forgiveness and salvation not only possible but actual and real. If it were up to us to make it real, we would have to save ourselves. We cannot save ourselves. Only God can save us (Matthew 19:25-26).

Every time Christ's forgiveness is proclaimed, it is the forgiveness of all our sins—past, present, and future. It would not be justification (acquittal) if we were still found guilty on some counts. Sins do not need to be forgiven over and over. But we need to be reassured over and over that they actually have been forgiven.

Forgiveness is a once-and-for-all matter, caused by Christ's sacrifice on Calvary. The means of grace, the forms of the Gospel, do not cause forgiveness. They do not turn away God's anger. That has already been done by our Lord. The means of grace merely—but really!—announce, proclaim, distribute, give, confer, and assure to us the grace and forgiveness already earned and won for us by Christ. The means of grace convince us of the forgiveness of sins. Christ authorized the preaching of this remission of sins in His name to all nations (Luke 24:47).

We still sin daily and much. Our sins pain and plague us. But God's grace is not interrupted by each sin so that we must somehow regain it. The grace of God is a constant even though we are variables. God is faithful. God does not change. By grace through faith we stand in the state of having been forgiven. We stand in the grace of God (Romans 5:1-2).

The forgiveness is not repeated. The message of the forgiveness is repeated—to convince and comfort, to assure and reassure us. It needs to be repeated for our sakes. It does not make God's grace more certain. It makes us more certain of God's grace. As a husband reassures his wife of his love, Christ reassures His church of His grace.

The sins that plague us are sins of weakness. Only Christians sin in that way. These sins are committed by believers without losing their faith in Christ. They are as dangerous and serious as ever. They are as strongly forbidden and condemned as ever. But the believer is not condemned (Romans 8:1). These sins are the violent lashing out of the Old Adam in his prolonged death throes (Romans 7:14-23).

The sins that cannot coexist with saving faith are sins of malice. They are malicious and willful. This malice or willfulness is a stubborn, hard-hearted, stiff-necked persistence in a conscious choice to disobey the will of God. These are the sins of unbelievers and only of unbelievers.

Sins of malice are not in themselves more serious than sins of weakness. The same sinful thought, word, or deed could result from weakness in one case and from malice in another. A sin could be outwardly more or less serious. It could be idolatry, adultery, murder, or speeding. If a Christian knows that a sin is a sin but chooses to prefer it to the grace of God in Christ, he has fallen from faith and so from grace.

Sin means the loss of God's grace in Christ only if it means the loss of faith in Christ. Every sin deserves damnation. Christ's obedience made up for our disobedience. Disobedience does not damn the one who repents for sin and trusts Christ for forgiveness. One who forgoes faith forfeits forgiveness.

Disobedience deprives the *former* Christian of salvation. It is not a degree but a kind of disobedience. The malicious sinner does not care about God's will and is stubbornly willing to offend God. He knows no Gospel motivation because he has rejected the Gospel. Where there is no faith in Christ, there can be no love for God. Where there is faith in Christ, there is the motivation to love God (1 John 4:19).

A Christian sins as a son. A non-Christian sins as a slave. The son wants a good relationship with the father he loves. The slave wants no relationship with the master he hates. The son is grieved by his disobedience and confesses it. The slave is pleased by his disobedience and conceals it.

A person cannot fall from faith through a sin of ignorance. A Christian who sins in ignorance has a weakness in knowledge or understanding. If he had known better, he might well have done better. Knowledge alone cannot keep an unbeliever from sin if he thinks he can get away with it. Education alone cannot make people better. They need conversion.

One falls into a sin of weakness. One dives into a sin of malice. The dive is intentional, eager, headlong and headstrong. A sin of weakness sneaks up on a Christian. A sin of malice makes a frontal assault. The new man strives and struggles against sins of weakness. Paul describes this constant conflict in Galatians 5 and Romans 7. After a sin of malice has been chosen, the new man is not there to resist. He has been murdered by the old man.

What is grace? Only the opposite of anger (wrath). The very word "grace" itself must mean the complete forgiveness of all sins, acquittal on all counts, all charges (Psalm 85:1-2; Romans 8:33).

How is grace merited, earned, won, achieved, brought about? Only by Christ's life and death for us, in our place, on our behalf, as our Substitute. He fulfilled the Law of God for us. He suffered the punishment for all our sins.

How is grace bestowed, conferred, given, assured to the individual? Only through the Gospel, but through the Gospel in all its forms (including Absolution, Baptism, Communion). The Gospel is God's Word, promise, and pledge of complete forgiveness for Jesus' sake. It assures and reassures us that our sins have been forgiven for Jesus' sake.

How is grace received? Only through faith, which is only the means of receiving (and the only means of receiving). The means of grace are God's means of giving. Faith is itself the reception of grace and forgiveness for Jesus' sake. Believing is receiving. That is the relationship between faith and grace.

How is grace lost? Only by losing faith, only by giving up that relationship to Christ. The person prefers sin to Christ. It is only by God's grace that you and I do not do so. If anyone loses faith, it is his own fault. We must not try to make that rhyme according to human reason! It cannot fit our natural way of thinking. But those are the facts of faith and unbelief (Acts 13:46-48). We leave the whys and wherefores up to God.

Faith can even be lost by "good works." Outward good works can be sins of malice if we hope and trust to earn God's grace by them. That view of good works would mean that one had fallen from faith in Christ and trusted himself instead. That is why Paul opposed the Judaizers (Galatians 5:1-4). If we try to save ourselves, if we trust our works instead of Christ's works for us, we have fallen from grace. Do not apply for the job of Savior. The position has already been filled.

In Luke 18:9-14, the Pharisee talked about his good works. The publican talked about being a sinner, in fact, in the original text, "the sinner," as if he were the only one. *The publican pled guilty and was acquitted.* The Pharisee pled not guilty and was convicted. His good works, like yours or mine if we want credit for them, are filthy rags (Isaiah 64:6).

Is faith conscious while we are asleep? Faith is not always conscious while we are conscious—nor should it be! While driving, our responsibility to God and man is to keep our eyes and our mind on the road. I would rather be operated on by a non-Christian surgeon who was thinking about his work than by a Christian surgeon whose mind was wandering in prayers and hymns.

God's grace in Christ is not interrupted when we are not thinking about it. God is thinking about it. He looks on us in grace for Jesus' sake. Grace is not an attitude in us but an attitude in God. His grace is constant. We stand constantly in it through faith in Christ (Romans 5:1-2), even when we are not thinking about it. The floor does not lose its reality because the people standing on it stop thinking about it.

Conversion and Baptism do not mean that we are ever after free of spiritual need. We need continual conversion. By the Word of God we need daily to stand beneath the cross of Christ, to see our sins condemned (Law) but especially to see our sins forgiven (Gospel). We do not daily lose faith and grace. But our faith needs strengthening and reassurance. That is the danger in sleeping late on Sunday or letting the Bible gather dust on the shelf. That is the danger in forgetting our Baptism or neglecting to prepare for Communion.

Because of Jesus there is no condemnation for Christians

(Romans 8:1). That is not hard for us to believe. It is impossible for us to believe. We need to be convinced by the Holy Spirit through the Gospel.

Romans 4:25 may be the most startling, most surprising passage in the Bible. It says that Christ was delivered on account of our sins and was raised on account of our justification. The Greek preposition as used there means "on account of," "because of." When translated "for," it sounds as if Jesus had been raised for the purpose of our justification. But the two prepositional phrases are parallel. That is clear even in translation.

Jesus was delivered to suffering, torture, and death *because of our sins*. He was raised *because of our justification*. He died because we had earned and deserved death. He rose because He had earned and deserved life for us. He rose because we had already been justified, forgiven, and acquitted because of His death in our place. Death was the penalty for all our sins. By His death Christ paid that penalty and paid it in full for all. Jesus could not be held in death (Acts 2:24). Christ's Resurrection proclaims our absolution, our acquittal, our justification.

That is the Gospel truth.

THE GOSPEL IN CONTEXT

In many "Lutheran" pulpits today the context of the Gospel is not preached. So the Gospel is not preached clearly if it is preached at all. Without context, how much content can be communicated?

The Law is the context of the Gospel as the problem is the context of the solution. The Law tells about sin. The Gospel tells about forgiveness. No one wants forgiveness unless he knows that sin is a real problem. Law and Gospel must be distinct, but they must be together. They must be preached in proper order. The Gospel must predominate. The Law must precede. The Gospel can be seen only against the background of the Law.

"Grace" may be the most misunderstood word of all time. The best way to define a word is often in terms of its opposite—provided that one understands the opposite. "Grace" is the opposite of "wrath" or "anger." The Law tells about the wrath of God because of sin. The Gospel tells about the grace of God because of the Savior. The grace of God in Christ simply means that because of Jesus' life and death for us and in our place, God is not mad at us any more. He is pleased with us for Jesus' sake. Every seven year-old child should be able to explain that.

The Law has three uses: (1) curb, (2) mirror, and (3) rule or guideline. The first use of the Law (curb) is the civil use, its application in external government. The home, the school, and the state must use force and punishment to curb external wickedness. The Gospel has nothing to do here.

The Gospel does not mean that a father should not spank a disobedient child. The Gospel does not mean that a teacher should not reprimand an unruly pupil. The Gospel does not mean that a judge should not sentence a murderer to death. He should (Genesis 9:6)! That is the first use of the Law, and the Gospel does not abrogate it.

The Gospel means that a *penitent* murderer can be assured that God forgives him because of Christ, and that he will go from gallows to glory, from cross to crown (Luke 23:40-43). But that comes after the Law has brought him to repent before God for his sin. That is the second use of the Law (mirror). The Gospel fits in between the second and the third uses of the Law. It comes after the Law as mirror and before the Law as guideline.

The second use of the Law (mirror) is crucial. The Law rightly accuses us of sin. It convicts us of sin and condemns us for sin because we are sinners. It is like the mirror that reveals a face in need of washing. The Law will accuse us of sin as long as we are sinners—throughout our earthly life. None of us can rightly hear any of the Ten Commandments without being convicted of breaking it.

The Law in its second use (mirror) is absolutely necessary before the Gospel. It is not necessary in a specific spiritual situation only if it has previously done its work. When a person confesses his sins, one should bring the Gospel without delay. The pastor will then refer to the Law only in that it is sin that is forgiven. He should preach only Gospel when dealing with a conscience troubled by the Law.

But most people today are not penitent. In our society one of the major attacks on the Gospel is the attack on the Law. People deny that sin is sin and so deny the need for Christ and His forgiveness. Many "Lutheran" preachers are not clearly condemning sin.

Many preachers pass over the Law quickly with a mere summary statement such as, "We are all sinners." That statement is true in and of itself. We have all said it. But it is sometimes said and often heard as a religious version of "Nobody's perfect." Then sin does not seem serious. But God did not speak meekly from Sinai (Exodus 19 and 20).

Many pastors do not preach "specific Law," as a layman I know has well said. The preacher must specifically condemn specific sins. It is easy to say, "I am a sinner," if one means, "I haven't always been the nicest guy in the world." That is not repentance. It is harder to say, "I am a sinner," if one means, "I have broken these Commandments, offended God Almighty, and deserved to suffer in hellfire forever." That is repentance.

Then comes the Gospel. The Gospel pardons the convicted sinner. The Gospel is not: "God is nice and loving and does not care that you sin." The Gospel is: "The sinless Son of God Himself bore the guilt of all your sin, suffered horribly for it, and paid your debt to God in full. He satisfied the wrath of God against your sin in your place by His death on the cross, and for His sake God forgives and pardons you and gives you eternal life and salvation." The real Gospel is meaningless to one who does not know the real Law.

The impenitent sinner pleads not guilty and is convicted. *The penitent sinner pleads guilty and is acquitted!* He is found not guilty because Jesus has already suffered the punishment. That is grace. That is forgiveness. That is justification. See Luke 18:9-14. The publican literally says: "God, be propitiated to me, the sinner." "To propitiate" means to make someone's attitude favorable by appeasing any and all anger. The publican refers to himself as "the sinner," as if he were the worst or even the only sinner. But he believes in Christ's sacrifice, the only sacrifice that propitiates or reconciles God to us.

The very same Law is applied in the third use (guideline). One who has known the bitter condemnation of the Law and the sweet consolation of the Gospel has a new attitude. The love of God in Christ moves the convert to begin to love God and to love Him more and more (1 John 4:19). The new man will want to do good and avoid evil (though in constant, internal struggle against the old man, Romans 7:14-25 and Galatians 5:17).

If you offend someone dear to you and really want forgiveness, you will appreciate forgiveness. Then you will try to be a better friend, a better husband or wife, a better son or daughter, in the future. If you were not really sorry but only wanted to smooth things over, you will only be glad that you have "gotten away with" something.

If one is aware of conviction by the Law and comfort by the Gospel, the guidance of the Law (third use) will be welcome. If one has not repented of sin or not believed the Gospel, instruction in the will of God will be unwelcome and unwanted.

The second and third uses of the Law bracket the Gospel. The Gospel looks back to the second use of the Law and is the forgiveness for wanting and doing evil. It looks ahead to the third use of the Law and is the motivation for wanting and doing good. It must always forgive because the Law always accuses. It must always motivate, not because subsequent holiness is a prerequisite for salvation, but because one who has known the horror of the Law and the comfort of the Gospel is moved to gratitude and needs guidance for a God-pleasing life.

There must also be "specific Law" as a guideline for holy living. Christians need specific guidance for the God-pleasing life. Otherwise they will get all kinds of silly notions into their heads, especially in today's topsy-turvy climate of moral confusion.

All too often a non-Christian hears about forgiveness for Jesus' sake and responds: "Well, then I can do as I please and sin as much as I want because it doesn't matter." The person has not been brought to repentance. He does not care about the Law as a guideline for holy living because he has not heard the Law as a mirror confronting him with the horror of his sinfulness. *Unless the Law has condemned sin and brought the individual to repentance, the Gospel will be heard as a license to sin.* That is why some people think that it is nasty to insist that Christians not speed, nor cheat on their taxes, nor live together without marriage.

A person who gets angry at the preaching of the Law has not accepted the second use of the Law (mirror). He does not want to admit his sins. He is fighting against acknowledging them. He is angered by being confronted with them. He still thinks salvation depends on his own performance and is terribly threatened by any implication that he might not measure up. He needs to be deprived of the hope of saving himself so that he can be given the hope of being saved by Someone else, namely by Christ.

The Law tells us that *because of sin we cannot save ourselves.* That is the bad news about our sin and God's wrath. The Gospel tells us that *because of the Savior we need not save ourselves.* That is the good news about our Savior and God's grace.

Notice how Law and Gospel are kept distinct in Romans. We are saved completely apart from our works, in fact, in spite of our works. Only then is there talk of wanting to do good and to avoid evil, not as a prerequisite for salvation but as a God-given response of gratitude for salvation already given and love for the Giver. Good works do not result in salvation. Salvation results in good works.

The distinction between Law and Gospel calls for constant study and reinforcement. Our Lutheran heritage is very helpful here. The three uses of the Law are a great aid in keeping things straight. All ideas of works righteousness must be kept out of the teaching of justification and salvation. Let us pray and labor for a return to true Lutheran preaching, which is true Biblical preaching, true Christian preaching. That is what we need to hear. That is what everyone needs to hear.

LAW AND GOSPEL

"For the wages of sin is death; but the gift of God is eternal life through Jesus Christ our Lord" (Romans 6:23). The greatest blessing of the Reformation is the clear preaching of the Gospel. For the Gospel to be preached clearly, the Law must be preached clearly. For Law and Gospel to be preached clearly, they must be kept distinct. Both Martin Luther (1483-1546) and C. F. W. Walther (1811-1887) were very clear about Law and Gospel. For both men, this clarity went back to their own experiences with the Word of God.

Both Luther and Walther, during their education, were taught works righteousness. In different ways, they were taught that they had to please God by doing the works of the Law. But through the Law, God taught Luther and Walther that the Law condemned their sins. The Law is the message of God's anger against our sin. But through the Gospel, God taught Luther and Walther that the Gospel forgave their sins. The Gospel is the joyous message of God's grace and favor in spite of our sin, because of our Savior. The Gospel is the good news that God has forgiven our sin because His Son, Jesus Christ, suffered and died for our sins in our place. Luther and Walther learned from the Bible that we have earned death, hell, and damnation by our sins. But they also learned from the Bible that forgiveness of sins, eternal life, and salvation are God's free gift for Jesus' sake. All their writing, preaching, and teaching were ever after characterized by the distinction between Law and Gospel.

Luther and Walther knew the terrors of conscience and the fear of God's anger against sin, anger that can mean only hell and damnation. Luther and Walther knew the comfort of the Gospel and the relief of God's forgiveness, favor, and grace for Jesus' sake. Luther read it in the Bible. Walther read it in the Bible and in the writings of Luther based on the Bible. Walther's long career as pastor and professor led to a series of practical presentations for seminary students about Law and Gospel. They were published after his death in the well-known book, *The Proper Distinction Between Law and Gospel* (trans. W. H. T. Dau, St.

Louis: Concordia Publishing House, 1929).

The distinction between Law and Gospel is not Walther's idea. It is not Luther's idea. It is God's idea. It is God's teaching in the Bible. It is basic to the whole Bible and to every part of the Bible. One of the briefest statements is our text: "For the wages of sin is death; but the gift of God is eternal life through Jesus Christ our Lord" (Romans 6:23).

The Law is the message that by our sins we have deserved God's wrath, temporal death, and eternal damnation. The Gospel is the message that Christ has, by His sinless life and by His suffering and death for our sins in our place, deserved for us God's grace, the forgiveness of sins, and eternal life. We believe Law and Gospel not because Luther and Walther taught them but only because God teaches them in His Word, His book, the Bible. Let us look more closely at the ways in which Law and Gospel are distinct.

We learn the Law and the Gospel differently. The Law is expressed in God's will in creation. It is written in the human heart. It is there to be read, though it is clouded over by sin. God gave us each a conscience. That is why even the non-Christian knows something of right and wrong apart from the Bible. Only from Scripture do we learn how deeply imbedded is our inborn sinfulness. Only from the Bible do we begin to see how thoroughly sinful we are by nature. Yet to preach the Law to an unbeliever, we are not telling him something that is completely foreign to natural human thinking.

But we learn the Gospel only from the Bible. It is completely foreign to natural human thinking. It is God's wonderful idea for our salvation. Only by the power of God the Holy Spirit do we learn to know and come to believe that our sins really have been forgiven by God for Jesus' sake. Only the Gospel brings us to and keeps us in the true Christian faith.

Law and Gospel have completely different contents. The Law is about us. The Gospel is about God. The Law is about our works. The Gospel is about Christ's works. The Law is about our sin. The Gospel is about God's Son. The Law shows us our sin. The Gospel shows us our Savior, Jesus Christ. The Law tells us what we are to do and not to do, how we are to be and not to be. The Gospel tells us what the Son of God, Jesus Christ, has done for our salvation.

The Law is the message of God's anger against our sin. The Gospel is the message of God's grace or favor for Jesus' sake. The Law says that God is mad at us because of our sins. The Gospel says that God is pleased with us because of our Savior. The Law condemns our sin and us. The Gospel forgives our sin and us. The Law is bad news. The Gospel is good news, the only really good news. The Law means death. The Gospel means life.

Law and Gospel have different promises. The Law makes promises only with conditions. The Law promises life and every blessing forever—to anyone who can earn it by living sinlessly, loving God totally, and loving the neighbor perfectly. There is only one problem. Since Adam and Eve, none of us has lived and loved perfectly. None of us has even come close. None of us has kept God's commandments. All of us have been born sinners and have been unable to help ourselves. All of us have sinned and sinned again. All of us have forfeited the promises of the Law.

The Gospel promises without conditions. The Gospel really has "no strings attached." Christ has kept God's Law for us. He had no sin. He lived and loved perfectly. But then Jesus, the eternal Son of God Who had also become true Man, became guilty in God's sight for all our sins. The Bible says, "The Lord hath laid on Him the iniquity of us all" (Isaiah 53:6). And "the wages of sin is death." Christ did die, horribly and torturously, suffering in our place for our sins. He died the death we deserved to give us the life He earned. There are no conditions. Jesus meant it when He said, "It is finished" (John 19:30). We do not save ourselves. Jesus has saved us. We are not our own saviors. Jesus is our only Savior.

Law and Gospel are different in terms of threats. Because we are sinful, the Law is full of threats. It threatens us with God's anger and all the punishment we have deserved by our sins. It threatens us with God's anger forever. It threatens us with pain and death in this world, pain and death in the next world. It threatens us with eternal, endless, everlasting torture in hell and damnation.

The Gospel knows no threats. It removes the threat of God's anger by proclaiming its opposite, God's grace in Christ. It removes the threat of punishment for sin by proclaiming forgiveness for Jesus' sake. It takes the sting out of pain and death in this world by removing the idea that God is mad at us and is punishing us. It removes the threat of death in the next world by assuring us of eternal life. It removes the threat of hell by promising heaven with perfect joy, with Jesus.

Law and Gospel have completely different results. Sometimes the Law makes people angry because they refuse to admit that they are sinners. They get mad when they are told about their sin. Sometimes the Law makes people despair because they conclude that God does not want to save them. They despair of being forgiven. Those reactions are not the fault of the Law but of the people who so react.

God's purpose with the Law is to bring us to repent. It brings us to acknowledge our sinfulness and our many sins. We admit to ourselves and to God that we are sinners and cannot save ourselves. The Bible says, "By the Law is the knowledge of sin" (Romans 3:20). This truth hurts, but it is necessary. We must know about the problem before we care about the solution. We must know about the question before we care about the answer. We must know about the disease before we care about the cure. We must know about the danger before we care about the rescue. We must know about damnation before we care about salvation. We must know about the Law before we care about the Gospel.

The first result of the Gospel is to bring us to faith in Christ, in the forgiveness He earned for us. The Gospel—the Word with the water in Baptism—gives us the new birth to the new life, the new spiritual life of faith. The Gospel in all its forms—including Absolution, Baptism, Communion —assures us of forgiveness, life, and salvation for Jesus' sake.

Through the Gospel the Holy Spirit gives us not only faith but also love, joy, peace, patience, and all spiritual blessings. Through the Gospel the Holy Spirit moves us to begin to love God and our neighbor and to grow in that love. By God's power faith in salvation leads to gratitude for salvation and also to love for the Savior and for those whom the Savior loves.

The Gospel assures us of forgiveness and moves us to love God and the neighbor. The Law gives direction to the love the Gospel creates. The Law gives us the specifics of how we should love God and the neighbor—but only the Gospel gives us the love. As gratitude and love grow by the Gospel, we do less and less evil, more and more good, by God's power, moved by the Gospel, guided by the Law.

Law and Gospel are for different people—or for the same people at different times. Everyone needs both, but in different circumstances. We always need to hear the Law because we are always sinners in this life. But the Law is especially and most importantly for those sinners who do not repent. It is urgent for them to be told of their sin and their need for the Savior.

The Gospel is only for those sinners who have already been brought to repentance. Forgiveness means nothing to one who does not know or refuses to believe that he is a sinner. One who does not repent does not want forgiveness. The most it can mean to him is that it is perfectly fine for him to go on living the way he has been. But to one who knows about sin, death, and hell, the Gospel means forgiveness, life, and heaven.

The distinction between Law and Gospel shows us how to read the Bible. Without this distinction the Bible seems to contradict itself. In the Bible, the Law condemns sinners. In the same Bible, the Gospel forgives sinners. We need to see and know that the Gospel is the message that Christ has delivered us from the curse of the Law. Whatever we read in the Bible, we must think in terms of Law and Gospel.

The distinction between Law and Gospel shows us how to teach. Every teaching of Scripture can be taught correctly only from this perspective. Our teaching always has the purpose of bringing people to repentance and faith. Consider teaching about God's power. Is God's power good news or bad news? If God is angry with us for our sins (Law), His power is bad news for us. We cannot escape punishment. If God is pleased with us for Jesus' sake (Gospel), His power is good news. He is always able to help and save us.

The distinction between Law and Gospel shows us how to preach. Law and Gospel, sin and grace, repentance and forgiveness, are the message that Christ wants proclaimed around the world to the end of the world (Luke 24:47). The pastor preaching in the pulpit, the layman sharing the Word privately, needs to know how God wants Law and Gospel used for the salvation of souls for whom Jesus died. We cannot use the Gospel to bring people to repentance. That is done only through the Law. We cannot use the Law to bring people to faith. That is done only through the Gospel. We cannot use the Law to motivate good works. That is done only through the Gospel.

The distinction between Law and Gospel shows us how to repent and believe. There is really no "how to" about it. We do not make ourselves repenters and believers. God does it through Law and Gospel. Through the Law He keeps us aware that we remain sinners in this life and that we need always to flee to the Gospel. Through the Gospel—including Absolution, Baptism, Communion—He reassures us again and again of forgiveness, life, and salvation for Jesus' sake. Through the Gospel He strengthens our faith in Christ and moves us to grateful love.

The distinction between Law and Gospel shows us how to face temptation. The Law condemns our sins. The Gospel forgives our sins. Aware of both as we are tempted to sin, the Law keeps us aware of our Father's and our Savior's will, but it is the Gospel that moves us out of grateful love to want to please God and do His will. When we do fall, the Law still condemns—but the Gospel still forgives—and lifts us up.

The distinction between Law and Gospel shows us how to pray. The Law shows us that we cannot approach God on the basis of our works. For our works are sin. The Gospel shows us that we may and should approach God on the basis of Jesus' works for us. We must not pray as the Pharisee (Luke 18:9-14), expecting God to bless us for our own sake. We should pray as the Publican, expecting God to bless us for Jesus' sake. We pray in Jesus' name, not in our own name. God will hear our prayers and will answer them in the way that is best for us.

The distinction between Law and Gospel shows us how to bear the cross, how to bear the loss of anything in this world, how to face trial, trouble, and tribulation. For we learn that, no matter how distressing, desperate, and dire things look in this world, we know that God is gracious to us for Jesus' sake. Because of Christ, God is pleased with us. No one and no thing can really, permanently, eternally harm us. We know from the Gospel, because of Jesus, in spite of all outward appearances, that God will turn everything to our benefit and blessing. In Romans 8, St. Paul lists everything up to and including death, everything in all creation, and says that none of it can separate us from the love of God in Christ. We know that only if, only as, we distinguish Law and Gospel—and emphasize especially the Gospel.

That is the final point. The Gospel must receive the greatest stress, the main and major accent. The Gospel must predominate. The problem is ours, our sin. The solution is God's, God's grace in Christ. We have the problem. We need to know about it. But most important for us is the solution. That is what we urgently, most urgently, need to hear and hear again.

The Law must be preached in all its bitterness, as if there were no Gospel. But then the Gospel must be preached in all its sweetness, as if there were no Law. From Mt. Sinai, one cannot see Mt. Calvary. From the perspective of the Law, there is no salvation. But from Mt. Calvary, one cannot see Mt. Sinai. From the perspective of the Gospel, there is no condemnation (Romans 8:1). It is the Gospel that must be heard loudest, longest, and last.

Let us remember always the bitterness of the Law and the knowledge of sin. But let us dwell on and ever return and run to the sweetness of the Gospel and the knowledge of our dear Lord and Savior Jesus Christ, Son of God and Son of Man, Who lived for us that we might not die, Who died for us that we might live, Who rose to raise us! Dr. Walther said to the future preachers, "God grant that some day people will say about you, that you are preaching well, but too sweetly!" *(The Proper Distinction Between Law and Gospel,* pp. 411-412). The taste of the Gospel is oh, so sweet! It will not fade away forever. Amen.

SURE SALVATION

A Roman Catholic priest was speaking about the Spiritual Exercises of Saint Ignatius. I wanted him to show his true colors. So I asked: "When people have completed these spiritual exercises, do you tell them to be sure of salvation or to doubt it?" He hemmed and hawed. Then he said, "We counsel prudential doubt."

That means: "We tell people that it is wise [prudent] to doubt salvation." Romanism teaches salvation by works. One must earn his way to heaven. In this life one cannot be sure that he has done enough. This doubt is supposed to move him to do more works.

The Biblical Gospel moves people to be sure of salvation. A person is saved by God's grace alone through God-given faith alone. God is gracious in spite of our sin, because of our Savior. Jesus Christ, the Son of God, died for our sin in our place and satisfied God's anger against all our sin.

If salvation depends on God, it is sure. If salvation depends on us, to any extent, it is unsure. In fact, it is impossible.

Romanism says that we must save ourselves but cannot be sure of doing so. The Bible says that we cannot save ourselves. Jesus Christ, true God and true Man, is the only Savior and all the Savior we need. God's Law tells us not to rely on ourselves for salvation. God's Gospel (good news) moves us to trust Christ alone for salvation (Romans 3:19-4:25).

Another Roman Catholic priest was speaking about justification. He said that Lutherans and Romanists today agree about the Gospel even if they differ about how to express it. So I asked: "Do current Roman Catholic theologians tell people that they can be sure of going to heaven when they die?" He said that, according to current Roman Catholic thought, one could not be certain of going to heaven, "not with the certainty of faith." Faith may be sure of other things, he was saying, but it cannot be sure of salvation. That is not the Gospel! That is not faith!

Someone asked me later whether that man could be a Christian. That was a good question. A Christian believes that his sins are forgiven for Jesus' sake. A Christian trusts that he has been saved by the life and death of the God-Man. Can anyone who holds the doctrine of doubt be a Christian? I said, "To the extent that he doubts his salvation, so do I."

We cannot judge anyone's heart. We hope that the man trusts Christ even though he cannot express the faith. But if he is a Christian, his faith is in great danger from the doctrine of doubt. That is not judging him. That is believing what he says about himself. The German text of the Apology of the Augsburg Confession says: "But dear Lord God, how may the people who still attack the teaching that we receive the forgiveness of sins through faith in Christ call themselves Christians or say that they have even once looked at or read the books of the Gospel?" *(Concordia Triglotta,* p. 166).

The Roman Catholic Council of Trent (1547-1563) condemned the teaching that a person could be sure of his salvation (unless he got a special message from God like the thief on the cross, Luke 23:43). It also condemned the teaching that we are saved by grace alone through faith alone *(sola gratia, sola fide,* Ephesians 2:8-9). The Council of Trent condemned the Gospel and rejected Christianity.

The Reformed are no better off. There are two kinds of Reformed theologians: Calvinists and Arminians. All teach doubt in one form or another.

Calvinists say that God actually wants some people to go to hell. One cannot be sure that God wants him to go to heaven. So one doubts salvation and looks in his life for evidence (conversion experience, good works) that he has been chosen for salvation. But he has no proof, no certainty.

Arminians (free will theologians, including Wesleyans and most Baptists) are like Romanists. They say that man is spiritually free and that salvation depends on him and his work in one way or another. Some may say "faith alone," but they make faith man's own work that saves him. That is faith in faith and faith in self. It is not faith in Christ.

Calvinism is like the sales gimmick that proclaims, "You may already be a winner." Arminianism is like the sales gimmick that proclaims a "free offer" but adds, "All you have to do is..." Both make salvation unsure.

Liberals of any denomination deny that the Bible is God's Word and go on to deny many, most, or all Christian doctrines. But Liberals, too, base their worldly salvation on human works to usher in an earthly kingdom of God.

Many of the Reformed are Christians. Many Roman Catholics are Christians. They trust Christ for forgiveness and salvation on the basis of God's Word in spite of hearing false doctrine. But they are in danger. Their doctrines tell them to look inside themselves for salvation. As long as we look at ourselves, our salvation is unsure.

The Bible tells us to look at ourselves. That is the Law! When we look at ourselves in the mirror of God's Law, we see only sin. The Law teaches the certainty of damnation. Then the Bible tells us to look at Christ. That is the Gospel! Without Christ, damnation is certain. With Christ, salvation is certain.

The Gospel directs us to look outside ourselves, to look at Christ. Jesus compared Himself to the brass serpent that Moses put on the pole (John 3:14-16; Numbers 21:4-9). The Israelites had been bitten by snakes. Those who looked within themselves to fight off the venom died. Those who looked outside themselves, at the serpent on the pole, lived.

We do not have within ourselves any spiritual resources that can save us. Those who trust themselves are lost. Those who trust Christ are saved. Christian faith is not faith in faith. Christian faith is not faith in the Christian. Christian faith is faith in Christ.

Only Lutheranism teaches the Gospel purely (those who do not proclaim it purely are not Lutheran even if they claim to be). We rejoice that there are Christians who are not Lutherans. Through the Gospel the Holy Ghost has brought them to believe the Gospel and trust Christ. But they are in danger in their fellowships, for they are told to look to themselves for salvation. We should be told to look to Christ alone for salvation.

Christian faith and hope are based only on Christ and the salvation He has procured for us outside ourselves. Salvation is brought to us from outside ourselves by God's Spirit through the Gospel in all its forms (including Absolution, Baptism, Communion). Dr. C. F. W. Walther said:

> "The characteristic feature of our dear Evangelical Lutheran Church is her objectivity, which means that her entire teaching is designed to keep man from seeking salvation within himself, in the powers of his nature and will, in anything he does or is, and to bring him to seek salvation *outside* of himself. The teaching of all other churches is of a subjective character; it trains man to base his salvation upon himself" (quoted in *Popular Symbolics,* ed. Th. Engelder (St. Louis: Concordia Publishing House, 1934, p. 5).

May God keep us faithful to the true Biblical Gospel to life everlasting. May He cause His Word to be proclaimed freely to the ends of the earth, to the end of the world. Amen.

THE FEAR OF THE LORD

Should we fear God? Some Christians will say yes and mean the right thing. Some Christians will say no and mean the right thing. Some non-Christians will say yes and mean the wrong thing. Some non-Christians will say no and mean the wrong thing. It depends on the meaning of the word "fear." A slave fears a cruel master. A son fears a kind father. The slave cringes in terror—akin to hatred—and is afraid. The son bows in respect—akin to love—and is not afraid.

Some non-Christians say that we should not fear God. Worldly modern people think that God, if He exists at all, does not care about sin. There is no need for fear—nor for forgiveness—because God was not angry in the first place. They are wrong. God is just. God is angry at their sin. They should be afraid. They should repent.

Some non-Christians say that we should fear God. They believe that God exists and that our relationship to Him is simply a matter of obedience or disobedience. They obey outwardly to some extent but only out of fear. They see God as severe Taskmaster and stern Judge. They need to learn the true meaning of God's Law. They need to be told the depth of their sinfulness, the total inadequacy of their merely outward attempts to obey God's Law. They should be afraid. They should repent.

By the Law, God brings people to repent, to acknowledge their sins against God, to know their need for forgiveness. By the Gospel, God brings them to believe, to trust that their sins have been forgiven because Jesus Christ, the eternal Son of God, died in their place for their sins. When they believe the Gospel, they are Christians. They will answer differently the question: should we fear God?

Some Christians say that we should not fear God. They mean that we should not be scared nor afraid of God, just as children do not shrink in terror from a loving father. That is correct. God's perfect love for us removes that kind of fear, for God loved us so much that He gave His Son to suffer and die in our place for our sin. The Gospel, the good news of forgiveness for Jesus' sake, removes our fear, for Christ has removed the need to fear—in the sense of terror, being scared or afraid. The Gospel gives us boldness and confidence as we approach God in prayer—or as we see our death and the end of the world approach.

Some Christians say that we should fear God. They mean that believers in Christ should still respect God, stand in awe of Him, and remember His justice, power, and holiness. God's love in Christ moves us to love God and to be grateful to Him—and to respect Him more than ever, in the right way. A child who knows his father's strength will be all the more grateful for his father's love, for being loved, forgiven, and welcomed into his father's favor. Our awe of God's power can only make us more grateful that He is gracious to us for Jesus' sake.

It is not easy to keep this straight. We are saints and sinners at the same time. The Law still terrifies us any time and every time we hear it—and rightly so, for we are sinners. Then and always we need the Gospel. The Gospel, the good news of forgiveness, life, and salvation for Jesus' sake, calms our fears, and takes away our terror—and rightly so, for we are saints. We are those whom God considers holy and sinless, perfectly innocent because Jesus Christ, true God and true Man, died for our sins in our place.

Should we fear God? The Bible seems to say yes and no. The seeming contradiction is removed if we remember the different meanings of the word "fear." We should not fear God with the fear of torture, torment, and terror (1 John 4:17-18). We should fear God with the fear of respect and awe (Psalm 130:4). We need to remember this distinction when we read Bible passages that speak of the fear of the Lord. Christians should fear God in a positive way, not in a negative way.

Should we fear God? The non-Christian should be afraid of God, with terror taught by the Law. Then his fears should be calmed by the Gospel. If he refuses to repent or, having repented, if he refuses to believe, he remains a non-Christian. He has not received forgiveness. He should still only fear God.

Should we fear God? The Christian should not be afraid of God. Though the Law has taught him terror, the Gospel has relieved that fear and replaced it with faith, trust, boldness, confidence in God's grace in Christ. God is no longer mad at us because of our sins. God is pleased with us because of our Savior.

Respect? Yes! Awe? Yes! Terror? No! Faith in Christ!

JESUS IS LORD!

People say, "You have to accept Jesus as Savior *and Lord!*" Aside from the proud, free-will implication of the word "accept," what bothers me is the emphasis they put on the term "Lord." They mean it in the sense of "boss" or "ruler." The idea is that for salvation it is not enough to trust Christ. One must also obey Him. They teach that we must do something to save ourselves by our own works. That is directly contrary to the Gospel (Ephesians 2:8-10; Romans 3:19-4:8).

When the New Testament calls Jesus "Lord," it means that He is true God. It means what the Old Testament means by "LORD," all in capitals. Compare Deuteronomy 6:4 and 1 Corinthians 8:6; Joel 2:32 and Romans 10:13. It is the name "Jehovah" ("He Who Is"), and it can be applied only to the true God.

The Septuagint was the Greek translation of the Old Testament done by Jews before the birth of Christ. It translated "Jehovah" as "Kyrios," "Lord." When the Greek New Testament says, "Jesus is Lord" (1 Corinthians 12:3), that means that Jesus is Jehovah, the only true God. Greek speakers familiar with the Old Testament could hardly fail to understand.

Greek speakers who did not know the Old Testament also knew that Jesus was being called "God." For them, "Kyrios," "Lord," was as strong a divine title as "Theos," "God." As they learned the Old Testament, this meaning was deepened in terms of the one true God.

But the Bible means still more by the term "Lord." It emphasizes the true God as the Savior and Redeemer. When He proclaimed the Ten Commandments from Mount Sinai, God did not start out, "I am the LORD thy God, so obey or else!" He said, "I am the LORD thy God, Which have brought thee out of the land of Egypt, out of the house of bondage" (Exodus 20:2).

The Israelites were to obey out of gratitude for delivery from slavery in Egypt—and for the promised delivery from sin and hell. We obey out of gratitude for the accomplished delivery from sin and hell. Both Testaments teach us to obey as loved and loving sons—not as threatened and fearful slaves.

A big book could be written about the Biblical use of "Lord." But even rapid Bible reading and quick word study show that, for Christians, the title "Lord" should be sweet and comforting. See how it is used in Psalm 9:1; 11:1; 18:1-2; 23:1; 27:1; 34:1; 103:1-22; and many more.

The same goes for the New Testament. In the opening greetings in his letters, Paul again and again connects "Lord" with grace and peace (Romans 1:7; 1 Corinthians 1:3; 2 Corinthians 1:2; Galatians 1:3; Ephesians 1:2; Philippians 1:2; Colossians 1:2; 1 Thessalonians 1:1; 2 Thessalonians 1:2; 1 Timothy 1:2; 2 Timothy 1:2; Titus 1:4; Philemon 3). That list includes every one of Paul's epistles. He cannot even get through saying, "Hello," before he connects the title "Lord" with the grace of God that the Lord Jesus earned for us by His suffering and death for our sin in our place.

Lutherans especially should know that "Lord" is a title of grace and peace, not dictatorial bossiness. For our pulpit greeting echoes Paul's prayer: "Grace, mercy, and peace be unto you from God our Father and from our Lord and Savior Jesus Christ." "Lord" and "Savior" are synonyms.

In his Large Catechism, Dr. Martin Luther sums up the second article of the Apostles' Creed by showing that "Lord" means "Redeemer." He writes:

> "But what is it to become Lord? It is this, that He has redeemed me from sin, from the devil, from death, and all evil" *(Concordia Triglotta,* p. 685). He says again: "Let this, then, be the sum of this article that the little word *Lord* signifies simply as much as Redeemer, *i.e.,* He who has brought us from Satan to God, from death to life, from sin to righteousness, and who preserves us in the same" (p. 685).

What should we mean when we say that Jesus is Lord? It should be our confession of faith that Jesus is our God, our Savior, our Redeemer!

TRULY THIS WAS THE SON OF GOD

"Truly This was the Son of God" (Matthew 27:54). These words were spoken by the centurion at the foot of the cross. He was the Roman officer in charge of the detail that crucified Jesus. Before Jesus was lifted up, the centurion knew little about Him. Before Jesus was taken down, the man had learned a lot. We do not know who the centurion was. Tradition says that he became a Christian and served as a pastor in Asia Minor. That may not be true, but it is possible. What a sermon he could have preached!

"Early that morning I learned that trouble was brewing. Pontius Pilate, the governor, wanted me and my men ready. A large mob had been gathered. The Jewish leaders knew how to turn out a crowd. The people were really stirred up, and I was afraid. Those Jews could be fierce when it came to their religion. And there were hundreds of thousands of people at Jerusalem for Passover.

"The first time I saw Jesus, He wasn't much to look at. He was worn out. He had been up all night and had already been tried and condemned by the Jewish court. He had also been beaten. His face and beard were bloody and sweaty. I can't say that I cared much about Him the first time I saw Him. Feel sorry for Him? Not me! To me He was just another trouble maker.

"I saw the strange trial before Pilate. I started to think there might be something wrong with what was going on. I'll say this for Pilate: he tried to be fair. He gave Jesus plenty of opportunity to speak in His own defense.

"The Jewish leaders had some serious charges against Jesus. Oh, we didn't care about their law. Blasphemy did not matter to Pilate! But we did care about people with political ambitions, especially if tax revenues were in danger. And nothing made Rome more nervous than the title 'king.' People remembered a line of bad kings from Rome's history. Even the emperors were not called 'king.' We let some local puppets use the title, but we made sure they were loyal to Rome.

"Still, Pilate saw through the plot. He knew that the Jewish leaders envied Jesus. He knew that Jesus was not guilty. How could that quiet Man be a threat to the might of Rome? Pilate said over and over that Jesus was innocent. He tried to shift responsibility to Herod, but Herod shifted it right back. They were so polite to each other! They were hardly polite to Jesus! Pilate wanted to wash his hands of the whole thing. He did wash his hands in front of the whole crowd to show them just that.

"The crowd forced Pilate's hand. That does not speak well for him. But he knew about mob violence. Even if he escaped with his skin, it would not look good on his record. So Pilate condemned Jesus, Who was innocent, and released Barabbas, who was guilty. Jesus was crucified instead of Barabbas. I had no idea that Jesus was also being crucified instead of me!

"I watched my men scourge Jesus. It was my job to make sure the scourging did not kill the Prisoner before He could be crucified. I decided when to stop the scourging, but I didn't stop it until Jesus' back was covered with blood. Then my soldiers mocked Jesus. They dressed Him up like a King. If only they had known! If only I had known! We crowned Him—but with thorns! The big thorns drew more blood.

"I saw Pilate show Jesus to the crowd and say, 'Behold, the Man!' I heard the mob shout, 'Crucify Him! Crucify Him!' I knew that it was going to be me that did the crucifying.

"I watched Jesus carry His cross. That was standard operating procedure. You didn't think one of us was going to carry that heavy thing, did you? I saw Jesus stumble and fall. I would like to think that I wanted to make it easier for Him. Maybe I was beginning to feel sorry for the Man. I knew He was innocent. But I had my orders! Isn't that a fine excuse? I obeyed orders I knew were unjust. But I didn't know Who Jesus really was, really is. Anyway, we got this guy from the crowd to carry the cross the rest of the way.

"I saw the soldiers lay Jesus down on the cross. I heard the blows of the hammer that drove the nails. I watched the body sag when the cross was raised. I looked at the terrible strain on His arms and shoulders and back. I saw what I had often seen—a Man dying a torturous death. But what a difference between Jesus and the others we crucified!

"My conscience bothered me. It was strange. I was not used to being troubled by any conscience. I heard Jesus say, 'Father, forgive them, for they know not what they do.' I asked myself, what was I doing? At that time I was more afraid of Pilate than of God. I carried out my orders. But I began to think about this Man Who called God His Father and asked Him to forgive us. Most criminals cursed us when we crucified them.

"About noon it got dark. The sun stopped shining. It wasn't

just cloudy. It wasn't an eclipse. The sun wasn't shining. People from other places remember it, too. The world was dark for three hours.

"Then I felt the earth quake. I saw tombs opened. I saw people climb out of them alive. I had heard Jesus cry: 'Father, into Thy hands I commend My spirit.' Again He had called God His Father! It scared me. But it made me think, too. I told the men, and anyone could have heard me say it, that Jesus was a righteous Man. But I knew that He was more than mere Man. I said that Jesus truly was the Son of God. The men were saying the same thing.

"I saw Jesus die. And He was dead. I know what a corpse looks like. One of my men stabbed Jesus in the heart with a spear. He was dead all right. I told Pilate that He was dead. Pilate told me to let Jesus' friends have the body. They buried it. They also knew that He was dead.

"Soldiers guarded the grave. But a few days later, the body was gone. Someone said the soldiers went to sleep on duty and the disciples stole the body. But if they had slept on duty, they would have died for it. No one laid a hand on them. It was all hushed up.

"I did not see Jesus after His Resurrection. But I heard His Apostles preaching that Jesus had risen from the dead. I knew it was true. God's Son would not, could not stay dead.

"I don't care what you think of me and what I did. I do care what you think of Jesus and what He did. I am here to tell you that Jesus was—and is—God's Son. I saw God die on that cross. That's as true as anything can be true.

"If I were the same person I was before that day, I would swear the strongest oaths I know that He truly is the Son of God. That's how sure I was of it then. That's how sure I am of it now, now that I have learned a lot more about Jesus from the Apostles.

"People ask me what I think about what I did. Well, I did wrong. Jesus excused it because we did it in ignorance. We didn't know He was God's Son. We didn't know that until we saw Him die. Sometimes my conscience bothers me for what I did that day. Pleading ignorance doesn't quiet my conscience, for I know that I have done a lot of other wicked things in my life and still sin a lot every day.

"Sometimes thinking about Jesus' death bothers me. But do you know what comforts me? The same thing: thinking about Jesus' death. Jesus was innocent, and all of us were guilty. Jesus was innocent, but He was the One Who was punished. All the things He said and all the things that happened that day mean what the Bible says: 'All we like sheep have gone astray; we have turned every one to his own way; and the LORD hath laid on Him the iniquity of us all' (Isaiah 53:6).

"Am I sorry for What I did? I'm sorry that I did wrong. But I'm not sorry that it happened. It was God's plan to save us. What happened there was our salvation.

"Thinking about Jesus' death and resurrection tells me over and over that my sins are forgiven. That's what I'm here to tell you—not only the fact that Jesus is the Son of God—but also the fact that He died to forgive your sins, too. That's what I'm going to tell people till the day I die.

"The last time I heard Jesus speak, I was His enemy. But He was my Friend. Thank God for His Word! Now I know that Jesus is my Friend—and that God the Father has a friendly attitude toward me because of Jesus. He has forgiven my sins for Jesus' sake.

"The last time I heard Jesus speak, I was His enemy. But He was my Friend. The next time I hear Jesus speak—whether I die first or He comes back first—the next time I see Jesus, He'll still be my Friend, and I'll be His friend forever."

What a sermon the centurion could have preached!

ON THE CROSS

The whole human race was represented on the three crosses of Calvary. The whole world was represented on the middle cross. There Jesus suffered and died for all, the only Substitute and Sacrifice for sinners. In another way, every one of us was also represented on one or the other of the two outside crosses. The men on both crosses were criminals and both reviled our Lord (Matthew 27:44; Mark 15:32). All people are sinners and by nature have no love for God. Like many people, the man on the one cross did not repent. Like some people, the man on the other cross was brought to repentance and faith (Luke 23:39-43).

The repentant criminal admitted that he deserved to be crucified. We should admit that we have also deserved that condemnation. Is that too strongly put? Have you and I actually sinned so seriously that we have deserved that horrible death? Why was Jesus on the cross? Not for anything He had done! But for everything we have done! He suffered our punishment there. We deserved that death. We deserved hell. He suffered it in our place.

The guilt of each criminal was the same. They were robbers and, probably, murderers. They were guilty of violent crime. Both of them initially insulted Jesus. The one who repented was not a better man. We are Christians, but not because we are in any way in and of ourselves any better than anyone else. We have deserved to be damned like everyone else.

One criminal was brought to repentance. Capital punishment confronted him with his evil life. God's Law, which he had heard before and which faced him now, brought him to repent and to acknowledge his sin. He cannot take credit for that. Nor can we take credit for the fact that God has brought us to know and admit our sin. Why did the other man not repent? Why do others not repent? That is their own fault.

Through the Gospel, the repentant criminal was brought to faith in Christ. Why had he heard the Gospel? He may have heard it before. But it seems that he at least heard Jesus say, "Father, forgive them" (Luke 23:34). That told him that Jesus was the sinless Son of God: sinless because He did not deserve crucifixion; the Son of God because He addressed God so intimately (the centurion also understood—Matthew 27:54; Luke 22:44). These words told him that Jesus was concerned to have people forgiven, not condemned. What more did he need to hear?

What the repentant criminal saw and heard, told him that Jesus was dying for him then and there, next to him but also in his place. The criminal died himself to pay his debt to man. Jesus died for him to pay his debt to God. Jesus' death paid our debt to God.

The repentant criminal confessed that Jesus was true God. He said that he and the other criminal were suffering the same sentence of death as—God! Jesus was dying the human death of God the Son. The repentant criminal called Jesus Lord and said that He had a kingdom. He knew that Jesus was and is the King of the kingdom of God.

The repentant criminal prayed to be included in Jesus' kingdom as a free citizen in good standing, with all his sins forgiven for Jesus' sake. Through all the pain attacking his mind, he saw that crucifixion was not the end for Jesus or for him. He still looked to the future, when the disciples had lost hope. He did not have time for a full adult confirmation course. But he understood some things more clearly than the men who had been listening to Jesus for three years.

The criminal who did not repent went from earthly torture to hellish torture. He has been suffering incredibly from that day to this. Death was no relief for him! We should not dwell on that unpleasant fact. But we should be grateful that Jesus has saved us from the same damnation. We should be moved to spread God's Word to save others, too.

The one who asked, received. Jesus promised: "Today shalt thou be with Me in Paradise." The repentant criminal went from earthly torture to heavenly joy. Since he was hanged on that cross next to the Lord, he has never been parted from the Lord.

The repentant criminal did not claim credit for his conversion. That was God's doing. Faith is being convinced by God, not deciding for ourselves, that Jesus suffered sufficiently to pay for our sins and earn our salvation. This man was convinced by God through seeing and hearing what we only hear about from the Bible. We are convinced and converted through the Word.

Salvation is entirely apart from good works on our part. The repentant criminal had done much evil. Now he could do no good. His hands were literally tied or nailed to the cross. He could not begin to make up for his crimes and sins. Neither can we! We owe God perfect love and obedience anyway. There is nothing we can do to make up for any failure to love and obey. By nature we cannot love God at all nor obey Him from the heart (Romans 8:7-8).

The repentant criminal spoke up for the Lord. That may have been a good work, proceeding from faith and love. But it was not what got him saved. What got him saved, and what gets us saved, is nothing that we do but everything that Jesus did and suffered for us. We are saved from our bad works apart from any good works on our part (Ephesians 2:8-9). The difference between us and that man is that most of us have more time and more opportunities on earth to thank God by doing His will (Ephesians 2:10). We have forever to thank and praise Him in heaven.

But the repentant criminal still hung on the cross. Jesus did not save him from earthly suffering and death. Like us, his conversion did not mean an immediate end to earthly trouble. Why did Jesus not do something to make it easier on the poor fellow? Both criminals lived and lingered longer on the cross than Jesus. The repentant criminal was a believer, a Christian. Why did Jesus not save him sooner, in some way, from earthly pain? If nothing else, why did Jesus not hasten the man's death?

The repentant criminal suffered yet for hours. Crucifixion was no picnic. A more cruel death has not been devised by man. Through dry and swollen lids, he watched a soldier approach with a heavy rod or hammer. Through dry and swollen lips, he screamed with what breath and strength he had left when his legs were broken. Guilty before man because of his crimes, he was righteous before God because of his Savior. Whether or not he used Jesus' exact words (Luke 23:46), he commended his spirit to the Father, Who was now his Father through faith in Christ (Galatians 3:26).

"We must through much tribulation enter into the kingdom of God" (Acts 14:22). God knows what He is doing and what He is permitting. It is enough for us that God knows why. We know that God is pleased with us in Christ, having forgiven us all our sin (2 Corinthians 12:9; Colossians 2:13). For us, God turns every curse into a blessing. If we do not now see how that is so, we will see when we look back later. When that repentant criminal stands whole and healthy, raised and glorified on the last day, he will have no complaints about the violence his body suffered on earth! It was better for him to meet Jesus, though it meant looking across from cross to cross, than to have gotten away with his crimes on earth and to be paying for them yet in hell. The same for us!

What strengthened the repentant criminal to bear the pain?

What gave him faith to believe and trust Jesus' promise of Paradise when there was no relief on earth? Christ gave him that faith through His Word: "Today shalt thou be with Me in Paradise." The Gospel strengthened and sustained him spiritually to endure the pain of the cross. The Gospel strengthens and sustains us spiritually to bear all the pains that we will suffer yet in this life, come what may.

It is wondrous that the repentant criminal did not lose his faith under all that he had to bear. God kept him in the one true faith. Jesus, even while His hands were nailed to the cross, did not let this man slip from His divine grasp (John 10:28-30). Jesus holds on to us, too. Otherwise we would be lost under far less torment than that repentant criminal bore.

What great joy, though in the midst of great pain, to have Jesus' precious promise, "Today shalt thou be with Me in Paradise"! What Jesus said to him, Jesus says to each of us: "Thou shalt be with Me in Paradise." He says that in the Gospel every time we hear or read or remember it. He says that in Absolution, Baptism, and Communion. He says it to us for the same reason He said it to that man. It is true because Jesus suffered and died in our place and completely paid for all our sins. It is said to comfort, strengthen, guide, and lead us gently, mightily home.

"Thou shalt be with Me in Paradise" is the same as "Thy sins are forgiven thee" (Luke 5:20). Our sins are forgiven for Jesus' sake. We will be with Jesus in Paradise. The only difference is that Jesus told the repentant criminal when, "Today." But that man already knew that he was dying soon. Unless the Lord returns first, we are facing death just as surely, though perhaps not as soon. Our comfort is that Jesus says to each of us, His redeemed and ransomed sheep and lambs, "Thou shalt be with Me in Paradise." He knows when. One day He will say, "Today," also to you and me. Amen.

PEACE, BE STILL!

Life is like being in a little bit of a boat on a stern and stormy sea. Wind and wave whip and wash over us. We must be ready for the going to be rough and tough.

We are battered and beaten by a thousand things: by international issues of war and waste; by noisome national news of crime and corruption; by hatred and horror against the most vital victims, children born and unborn; by screaming scandals of immorality and indecency; by moral pollution and perversion pervading the peoples; by worry at work; by stress at school; by hassle at home; in short, by trials, troubles, and tribulations.

The disciples on Galilee were in no strange situation when that sudden storm arose (Mark 4:35-41). Jesus' disciples frequently face powerful pressures. The Apostle Paul informed recent converts: "We must through much tribulation enter into the kingdom of God" (Acts 14:22). We all have personal problems, from certain secret sins to daily dilemmas to immense and impending fears for the future.

With all our worldly worries, we wonder whether Jesus is again asleep. He slept soundly in that sinking ship, His facial features calmly composed on a pillow. He was not worried. The disciples cried and called as we are tempted at times to do: "Master, carest Thou not that we perish?"

Of course, Christ cares! The Lord loves us. He will help, but He need not hurry. He lets a bit of bilge build up in the bottom of the boat. No matter for the Master! We wade through worries and woes. We doubt but that our distresses should get daily deeper. No problem for the Prince of Peace!

Jesus just stands still and stable and solid in the midst of all that motion and commotion. With wonderful words He whisks away the wind and wipes away the wave. He calls for complete calm, and all the elements obey. He says, "Peace!" And there is perfect peace. He says, "Be still!" And all is quite calm and quiet.

The disciples were impressed by Jesus' power. The Master's might made them fearful and frightened. They asked, "What manner of Man is This, that even the wind and the sea obey Him?" We might well worry about this Person's power because our sins are certainly serious. But we need to know that Jesus' power is for our peace! His strength is for our salvation! He is no mere man. He is God, the Son God, the great God, the only God, the almighty God. But the Lord is love! The Sovereign is our Savior! He fights our foes and fends off our fears.

Jesus holds out hope for help. This hope is not human but heavenly. It is based and built solely and solidly on Jesus Christ, on His life in light and His death in darkness. For His death is our life; His doom, our hope; His cross, our comfort.

Jesus lived the life that we should have lived. He loved as we should have loved. He obeyed as we should have obeyed. And then He died the death that was our due. He was doomed for our disobedience. He ended God's anger against our sin. He earned eternal life for us. God has forgiven and forgotten our sins forever for Jesus' sake. Because of Christ, God is gracious to us.

Because of God's grace in Christ, the Master's might gives us faith to face the future. We know we need not fear nor fret. Jesus loved us long ago, and He loves us lastingly, everlastingly. Our troubles are temporary. Our pains are presently past.

The disciples doubted then. Their faith was far from firm. But Jesus guarded and kept them. We are weak. It may be that we doubt daily. But Jesus loves and leads us nevertheless.

Our troubles and turmoils will soon enough subside. For Jesus, our God, will soon enough decide to say once more: "Peace, be still!"

Then we will wonder why we were worried. Our Lord said to the disciples whom He had recently rescued: "Why are ye so fearful? How is it that ye have no faith?"

Jesus' majesty and might are combined with care and concern. As prominent as is His power, so great is His grace and goodness toward us.

Our fears will be forgotten. Our faith will be confirmed. Our doubts will be destroyed. All anxieties are banned and banished by the simple sound of Jesus' winning words: "Peace, be still!"

FEARS, TEARS, AND YEARS

A child wakes in his crib, alone in the nursery. He is hungry and afraid. He does not know where his next meal will come from. He cries. His mother is well within earshot, attending to housework or resting for a few moments. But he does not know that. For all he knows, his mother is no longer alive or no longer exists at all. He is afraid. His mother quickly comes to comfort, tend, feed, and nourish him. He need not have been afraid.

A baby must learn that people and things do not cease to exist just because they are outside his field of vision. We need to learn to remember that God still exists, even though we cannot see Him, even when we cannot perceive how He is helping, blessing, and caring for us. We need that awareness when we are afraid, whenever we cry out in the darkness of this world.

A child weeps because his request has been denied or his pleasure delayed. The most minor of losses causes him to despair of ever again experiencing peace, contentment, joy. He cannot look beyond his most immediate needs or wants. That takes years to learn.

A youngster must learn to accept disappointment. He must bow to the superior wisdom of his parents. He must trust that, when they deny him something, it is for his own good. They know that it would be bad for him—or not as good as what they are preparing instead. We need to learn the same things. As much wiser as human parents are than their children, our heavenly Father is infinitely wiser yet. If He says no, it is because He plans to say yes at a better time or because He is preparing something good for us in place of something bad we want—or because He is preparing something better for us than even something good we want.

A child waits so impatiently. Only a few minutes into an hour-long trip, he asks, "Are we there yet?" So little time has passed in his life compared to the years of an adult, that he cannot fathom that an hour will pass quickly enough. When he is told he must wait, an hour seems an eternity. The few days or weeks until birthday or Christmas seem forever and then some.

A child must learn that time does pass. And with it pass away the things that hurt and harm and pain us in this life. Eagerly anticipated joys do finally come. But then, if they are earthly joys, they pass away, too. Waiting is hard. Waiting patiently is impossible without hope assured and reassured. But the hope of eternal life for Jesus' sake is the most certain of all hopes. It will not be disappointed because Jesus' life and death truly have earned for us the forgiveness of sins, eternal life and all the blessings of salvation. Those joys last forever.

A parent tells a child to wait: "It's only an hour." God tells us to wait: "It's only a lifetime." The few short years we spend on earth are nothing compared to eternity. A child's petty, petulant pouting when made to wait is really very much like our throwing before God a thousand whys while we wait for His help in our earthly needs and for the bliss of eternal life.

A well-read woman, all-too familiar with the varieties of human religion, still searching for something solid, asked me: "What's the hook?" At first I did not understand what she was asking. She was asking for something to hold on to. She wanted to know what made sense out of all our problems on this earth and the many ways in which they seem to contradict faith in God.

The "hook" is Jesus. The Son of God became Man not to abolish the sorrow of this world in this world but rather to share that sorrow with us, for us, and, most importantly, in our place. God and Man in One, He lived our life and died our death. The life we should have lived, He lived. The death we should have died, He died. All the guilt of all our sin, all the anger of God against our sin.

All the guilt of all our sin, all the anger of God against our sin, He took upon Himself and slew it by His death. He earned for us the complete forgiveness of all our sins. He won for us the grace of God, peace with God, joy in God, and the hope of everlasting life before God's smiling face.

Because of all Jesus did and suffered for us; through the faith, hope, and trust in God worked in us by the message of Jesus, the Gospel; our fears, our tears, and our years lose their sting. They cannot deprive us of comfort, assurance, peace, and joy in the secure knowledge of eternal salvation for Jesus' sake—and of God's help along the way in ways we cannot now fully comprehend.

When we look back from the eternal maturity of glory, we will realize how silly and childish we were in this life. But we will not regret that we were like children in one way—in the comfort we were granted by our Father's hand holding ours, our Father's arms holding us—in Christ, through His Word.

THE LONG HAUL

How often does any one thing make a big difference in a person's life? Little things are always making little differences. But big things that make big differences are few and far between. Most big differences are accumulations of little differences.

A major crisis is rare. If crises were happening all the time, there would be too much history to write. Actual turning points for people or groups of people occur seldom enough that they can be isolated and analyzed.

Crises are critical. But they are not the whole story. Short steps cover long miles. Many little turns outweigh spectacular events. Most important work is dull. Progress occurs inch by inch.

In Christianity, conversion is important. But perseverance is just as important. "In your patience possess ye your souls," said Jesus (Luke 21:19). We commemorate birth, but once born we need daily bread. We remember Baptism, the washing of regeneration (John 3:5; Titus 3:5). But having been born again, we need the Word of God and the Lord's Supper frequently to nourish spiritual life.

The Christian life is a marathon, not a sprint. For some people, it may be a short dash to the finish line (a deathbed convert, the penitent thief on the cross, the Christian child whom the heavenly Father takes home). But for most of us, endurance is more important than speed. "The race is not to the swift" (Ecclesiastes 9:11).

The Christian life is a war, not a battle. It is not one fight or confrontation that is soon done. It is a long series of battles, some large, many small. All are mortal combat.

It may be news to some people, but the struggle with the devil, the world, and the flesh does not get easier. It often gets harder and more complicated, like the long distance runner's battle with fatigue. A soldier's last battle is no less frightful than his first.

The old Adam in us should, as Luther's Small Catechism says, "be drowned and die" through daily application of Law and Gospel. But as someone said about the old Adam, "That guy can swim!" A lifeguard will tell of the strength and violence of a drowning man.

Many young Christians are idealistic. Their spiritual energy seems as boundless as their physical energy. They have not yet faced prolonged trial, trouble, tribulation, and temptation. Some fall away when the going gets tough ("which for a while believe," Luke 8:13).

But are we not supposed to grow better and stronger in our faith? Should that not be part of maturity? Well, yes, but! Many Christians feel worse and weaker as they grow older, or as some severe temptation grows longer. They are not weaker, only wearier, like the long distance runner approaching the end of the race. The last mile, the last lap is the hardest.

The middle of the race is hard enough. Many a believer wonders how he can go on. The weariness is not evil. Some coaches say about workouts, "No pain, no gain." There is some truth to that. The work that wears a person out is necessary if he is to be built up. But it must be combined with proper nourishment. Spiritual exercise does not make us stronger. It puts to use the strength we received from Word and Sacrament. It also teaches us the uselessness of any other supposed source of strength.

Veterans of the cross may have more, not fewer, spiritual aches and pains. They may carry many scars from many wounds. Total healing is not here, but there! Health is in heaven. Old soldiers are not worse soldiers, nor are they any less brave and loyal, for all they suffer. They are but closer to the heavenly retirement, which God well knows when to grant. We will not be overstressed (1 Corinthians 10:13).

The point is to keep the eyes of faith fixed on the heavenly goal. The only way to do that is the Gospel, the message of full pardon and free forgiveness of all our sins because of the life and death of God's Son, Jesus Christ, in our place. Because of Jesus, we are assured of crossing the finish line, winning the war, going to heaven.

That is not at all because of our efforts. That is entirely because of Christ's efforts on our behalf. When the angels usher us into glory, we will know why we had to face such wearying warfare, such agony of endurance (Acts 14:22). We will know then, better than ever, that our salvation is entirely God's doing. Yet we will not regret the fear and trembling along the way (Philippians 2:12-13).

THE ROAD TO CAPERNAUM

The Gospels are tantalizing. We want to know so much more, so many human interest details. We must be content with what we have. In His Word, God has given us all the information we need. If the Bible answered all our questions, we would not be able to carry it around, not even in a big truck (John 21:25). In heaven there will be no end of time to talk to the saints.

One intriguing character is the man from Capernaum (John 4:46-54). He travelled several hours to Cana to ask Jesus to come to Capernaum to heal his son. Jesus healed the boy without leaving Cana. The man went home to find his son well.

The original text calls this healing a sign (v. 54). It was a clear indication that Jesus is true God. Who but the Creator could heal with a word spoken at a distance? Who but God has that unlimited power and that unlimited presence?

The main meaning of the sign is the identity of Jesus as true God. That is the primary point of all the miracles. But there is often a poignant, personal point, too. In this case, the faith that Jesus gave this man is interesting and instructive.

It is not surprising that the man believed after he saw that his son was well (v. 53). Jesus complained about people needing signs to believe (v. 48). But this man also believed before he saw. He believed the Word of Jesus (v. 50). Jesus gave him that faith through that Word.

Knowing Who Jesus is, there is no reason not to believe. Jesus said, "Thy son liveth," and the son lived. That was the same as when God said, "Let there be light," and there was light (Genesis 1:3). Jesus is God Almighty.

But the man did not see right away. He had faith without sight, before sight. We have not seen yet at all. But we have believed—by God's power through His Word (John 20:29). We walk through life as that man travelled the road to Capernaum— by faith, not by sight (2 Corinthians 5:7).

The man had to wait. He could not phone home. He could not race there in a car. What did he think every step on the road to Capernaum? What do we think every step of the way through this world and this life?

It was late enough and far enough that the man did not get home until the next day. Did he spend an anxious evening, a sleepless night? He was concerned. He was eager to see his son. He need not have worried. But he was weak. His faith was not perfect. He still struggled with doubt. But he probably slept (Psalm 127:2).

We still struggle with the sins of doubt and worry. Our faith is weak. But Jesus is not weak. His Word and His promises are certain. Because He died for our sins in our place, we have God's grace, the forgiveness of sins, eternal life, and salvation. It is enough for us that God is pleased with us for Jesus' sake. That is all we need (2 Corinthians 12:9).

How happy that man was when he got back to Capernaum! How happy we will be when we get to heaven! Looking back on the road, we will know that we need not have been anxious at all about anything. Since we know now what we will see then, let us not worry. Let us trust—because of Jesus' death, because of Jesus' life, because of Jesus' power, because of Jesus' promises, because of Jesus!

THE TINY CASKET

The open casket was two feet long. The date of birth and the date of death were the same.

The mother wept. The father wept. The pastor wept.

"He has curly hair," said the mother.

"He'll never catch a ground ball," said the father.

"You can't take care of your baby," said the pastor. "But Jesus can."

"I have to believe that," said the mother.

That really happened. With different details, it has happened many times.

The baby's life was short: nine months. There is nothing to do but trust the Lord. That is always the case, for every one of us.

Every human death is a tragedy as far as we can see on earth. But the Lord can see further than we can.

Jesus died for original sin as well as actual sin. Jesus died for infants as well as, as much as, for adults. Jesus died for all.

By the grace of God in Christ, we hope and trust that the baby's life is as long as eternity. That is the only hope for any of us. But that is great hope!

There are other stories of other people: the doctor who blamed himself, the parents who did not come to church, the sister who lived—but without water and the Word.

The Lord always knows what He is doing and why. It may be that He snatched that little boy from the greatest danger. We trust God's wisdom, power, grace, and love in Christ. That is all there is to say. That is enough.

A TREE GAVE ITS LIFE

Does getting closer to nature bring us closer to God? Many poets have said so. But it is not always true.

If we enjoy the great outdoors without the Word of God, we are not getting closer to God. We are getting further away from Him.

If we enjoy the great outdoors with the Word of God—in our hands and in our hearts—we see things differently. Consider a tree.

A tree is pretty to look at and nice to sit under. A tree gives us fruit to eat and air to breathe. In death, a tree yields warmth and light as firewood and sturdy material for houses and furniture. This is printed on paper made in part from the corpse of a tree.

But a tree is so much more when viewed from the high perspective of God's Word.

In its beauty and its fruit, a tree reminds us of the power and wisdom of God in creating this world and of the love and goodness of God in preserving it.

But it was by a tree in a garden that man first disobeyed God. It was by eating the fruit of a tree that man brought sin, death, and misery into the world. A tree reminds us of our sin and our sins and our sorrows.

The greatest glory of wood is that our Lord Jesus Christ, the Son of God and Son of Mary, was nailed to the tree of the cross for our salvation. He died on a dead piece of wood for us to live. He died there for our sins in our place.

A tree gave its life so that He could give His life—to give us eternal life. The fruit of that dead wood surpasses the fruits of all other trees that have been or will be. That fruit is the grace of God, the forgiveness of sins, the joy of heaven for all believers in Christ. A dead tree and an instrument of death, the cross still yields life—eternal life.

Will heaven be treeless? It was not that way in the vision that God gave John (Revelation 22:2). May those who wander in the woods of this world—dark forests indeed—be gathered in heaven beneath the tree of life— through faith in Him Who died on the tree of the cross.

DIMENSIONS OF LOVE

Have you ever swum in the ocean? It is very impressive. There is no comparison with a pool, a lake, or even one of the Great Lakes. The first time I swam in the Atlantic, I was awed by its sheer vastness. On this side was Florida! On that side were Spain and Portugal!

The dimensions of the Atlantic! From the Arctic to the Antarctic. From the Old World to the New. Its waves lap shores from Canada to Capetown, from Trondheim to Tierra del Fuego. Its depth can be measured in miles, harboring the Titanic and so many others.

Yet the Pacific dwarfs the Atlantic in breadth and depth. If Mt. Everest were sunk in the Marianas Trench, its peak would be a mile under water. The distinction between the oceans is artificial. They are really one huge sea.

In Ephesians 3:14-19, St. Paul writes that he prayed for the Christians to understand the dimensions of God's love in Christ. God's love is great beyond all our thinking or imagining. Its breadth knows no bounds; its length no limits; its height and depth, no end.

How great is the love of Christ for us? It reaches from the height of heaven to the depth of death. God loved us so much that He sent His Son to suffer for our sin, to die in our place. God Himself paid the debt we owed Him for all our sins of every size and shape, of every description and dimension.

God's love is so great that all the atrocities of human history could not dim, dull, dampen, or diminish it. God the Son willingly came to live our life and die our death. He rose and lives to give us life in spite of death. He sent His loving Spirit to convince us of His love through His Word of love.

Jesus loves sinners! He did it all for us not because we were good, but because we were bad; not because we loved Him, but because we hated Him; not because we had done anything for Him, but because we had done everything against Him; not because we deserved salvation, but because we deserved damnation; not because He needed us, but because we needed Him; not because we wanted Him, but because He wanted us.

There is no greater height of love nor depth of caring. It is beyond our ability to grasp. But let us also remember its length and breadth. The length of His love extends over the whole world. He died for all, absolutely all people. He died for the people who commit the worst horrors you have ever heard.

Jesus died for the worst sinner I know. He died for me. Jesus died for the worst sinner you know. He died for you. For each of us has more information about his own sins than about anyone else's. But that need not matter any more. All is forgiven. Christ died for us.

How can we not love Him—though our love can never compare to His—and how can we not love all those for whom He died?

ACCEPTANCE AND FORGIVENESS

Television programs and newspaper articles often deal with the problems of teenagers. We hear again and again what we have heard before. Teenagers need to be accepted but feel pressured to succeed. They fear that they will fail and be rejected.

People of every age are in that situation. We need to be accepted by other persons. But society pressures us to achieve "success," whatever that is.

It gets complicated. We begin to fear rejection in case of and because of failure. The pressure increases when personal worth is based on achievement. Our value, even in our own eyes, comes to depend on some idea of performance.

What are we to do? We can work like mad to achieve success. But that effort is doomed to failure, eventually, for everyone. Even those who succeed most in worldly terms are not satisfied. They still want more and more success.

Or we can struggle to be free from mental and emotional slavery to success. We can view our worth—and the worth of others—as a reality with or without money, fame, beauty, power, or any of the elements that spell "success" in the world.

Do not misunderstand. We should work hard and do our best to be helpful in family and community. But our sense of worth and our acceptance by others should never depend on what we do but only on what we are— human persons created by God, loved by God, redeemed by God.

The point is to take the pressure off. But can it be done? In a world of sinners like us, this pressure remains rather constant. The only way for such acceptance to survive is for forgiveness to occur—and recur. We all do things that are wrong. We all disappoint ourselves and others. We need forgiveness. That is the only way for acceptance to endure.

What is forgiveness? It is not: "No harm done," nor, "It doesn't matter." That denies that anything is or was wrong. That is condoning, not forgiving.

Forgiveness is: "You did wrong. I was angry. But I never stopped loving you. I have forgiven you. I am not angry any more." Forgiveness is acceptance in spite of wrongdoing (or wrong-saying, or wrong-thinking, or wrong-being).

Christianity is the religion of forgiveness and acceptance by God. Other religions tell us that we can do enough good works to make God like us and accept us. Christianity admits that we are sinners and that sin is seriously wrong.

But God loves us in spite of our sin! God the Father sent His Son to be our Savior. Jesus suffered God's entirely justified anger against our sin. He satisfied that anger for us. He appeased it by His pain and death.

The message of Christianity is that God forgives and accepts sinners. He welcomes believers as His children for eternity—in spite of sin, because of Christ!

God is at work in His word to convince us that He really has forgiven our sins for Jesus' sake. It is not based on anything we do. That forgiveness is the only really powerful motive for us to forgive and accept others also.

OF SPACE AND SALVATION

On a trip to Florida, I toured Kennedy Space Center. The distance I travelled to get there seems insignificant compared to the long space flights that have begun there. It is an impressive place.

The moon missions and the shuttle flights are amazing technological achievements. But there was an epic journey on a much greater scale, far beyond all human flights—of fact or fancy—combined. That was the journey of Jesus.

Astronauts have bridged the distance from the earth to the moon. Jesus has overcome the separation of sinful, finite man from the infinite, holy God. For He is God the Son become also a true Man, yet without sin.

Given time, leisure, and the right books, most of us could understand most of the working of space flight. But we cannot comprehend how God became Man. That is something only God could know and plan and do.

The cost of space flight is enormous. But the cost of Jesus' journey was infinitely greater. The cost was the suffering and death of God's own Son for our salvation.

The weight of the rockets and their payloads is hard to imagine. It runs into millions of pounds. But Jesus' burden is inconceivable. He bore the load of all human guilt, the weight of all our sin.

We may think of Jesus coming down and the astronauts going up. But Jesus also journeyed uphill—up Mt. Calvary—carrying His cross and our sin. He descended to the grave and to hell. He also rose from the dead and ascended into heaven. No one else has done anything comparable.

Much is accomplished by what the astronauts do. Infinitely more is accomplished by what Jesus suffered to be done to Him.

The technical complexity of the space vehicles is astounding. But so much more has been accomplished by the simple wood and nails of Jesus' cross. Our whole debt to God has been paid in full. Those few feet of wood cast a longer shadow than the towering metal structures of Cape Canaveral.

NASA means something. INRI—Jesus of Nazareth, King of

the Jews— means everything.

A few people have been in space for short periods of time. A few more are preparing for other brief, dangerous trips. But many—all believers in Christ—have a safe ride from earth to heaven in the arms of the angels. That is much greater than a trip to the moon. They will remain in joy and freedom in God's presence forever. That is much better than a few weeks confined in a cramped capsule.

I have tasted neither the plastic-packaged space meals nor the heavenly banquet spread. But I know which is more to be savored.

Astronauts must be highly qualified and meet rigid standards. Christians admit that they are not at all qualified for heaven. But Jesus has met the standards for them. NASA may not be willing to accept you for space. But God is willing to accept you for heaven—because of Jesus.

Man wrongly claims the credit, the glory for space flight. God rightly claims all credit, all glory for salvation. To God alone be glory forever! Amen.

COMBINED PARABLES

Jesus' agricultural parables have lost none of their relevance on the mechanized modern farm. I contemplated that fact recently while harvesting corn with a combine worth about six years' salary. It may have been risky for the farmer to trust me with the equipment and the crop. But in spite of my inexperience, an amazing amount of corn went into the hopper and then into the truck.

I saw this year's crop through all the stages of growth: "First the blade, then the ear, after that the full corn in the ear" (Mark 4:28). Jesus was not speaking directly about our American corn, but the words still fit. Modern machinery does not alter the growth process. All the farmer's investment of work and worry, time and money, does not change the fact that he must wait on events beyond his power to control or understand (Mark 4:27). No amount of worried weather watching will help the crop grow. But the farmer knows when it is time to harvest (Mark 4:29).

The kingdom of God is like that. We cannot control its growth. We fret in frustration as we want to accomplish this or that for the kingdom. Forget human thinking and human doing! We cannot bring about anything spiritually good by our work or effort. God's goals will be accomplished by His power through His Word. His heavenly harvest, the crop He wants, will be ready for reaping at the right time.

Harvesting with a combine is violent. The combine reminds me of a surrealistic tank in some science-fiction movie. At the front are six huge points that seem like armored rams. The points separate the rows of plants and guide the stalks toward fast-moving chain-link grippers that jerk them downward. That bounces the ears back to a whirring, whirling augur that sweeps them into a mysterious mouth that swallows them to a horrible grinding digestion. Miraculously the kernels are whole when another augur tosses them into the hopper behind the cab.

All this marvelous machinery does not alter the principle: "Whatsoever a man soweth, that shall he also reap" (Galatians 6:7). Harvesting with a combine, one sees not only what was planted but also what weeds have grown with the crop (Matthew

13:7, 26). One sees how straight the rows were planted. If they are not straight, the corn stalks wave futilely before being jerked down to doom. Do what he will at harvest, the farmer cannot change the crop. It is what it is and where it is. What it is good for and where it is going have long since been determined.

It is too late for tender loving care. As my farmer friend said about the combine, "It has no mercy." Nor will God have mercy on the tares, the weeds, or the chaff on Judgment Day (Matthew 13:12; 13:30). When Jesus judges, the Christian believers will hear only about the good works that God has done through them. Their sins, having been forgiven, are no longer on the record (Matthew 25:34-40; Ezekiel 18:22). But the non-Christians, no matter how they may have deceived men about the state of their souls, will hear only about their sins (Matthew 25:41-45).

Combines harvest faster than hands. But harvesting still seems slow. I kept the combine moving about 2.5 miles per hour, slower than a steady walk. Compared to driving a car, it was like crawling. But as slow as the combine went, it was moving faster than the corn! The word "inexorable" seems most fitting for its progress and process. So is God's work. It seems slow, for we are eager to be taken to heaven. We wonder why judgment is delayed (1 Peter 1:3-9; 2 Thessalonians 1:3-10). But God is working and moving at the right pace for us.

Once the combine grabs the stalk, fast and furious things begin to happen. As slow as the going seems now, Christians know that God knows the best time for everything. The eternity of God's joy will make our little while of waiting more than worthwhile. Current crises cannot compare to the Christian's everlasting glory (Romans 8:18). Those who have not been converted will hardly think that they have had enough time. "Too late" will seem too soon to them. God is right about time in their case, too, "For they shall soon be cut down like the grass" (Psalm 37:2; read the whole psalm).

The parable that is most on my mind after combining is the Parable of the Wheat and the Tares (Matthew 13:24-30; 36-43). God will sort things out, through His angels, separating the wheat and the weeds. In those terms, or in terms of threshing and winnowing (Matthew 3:12), or in terms of separating sheep and goats (Matthew 25:31-33), the point is the same. God will completely and finally separate Christians from non-Christians on the Last Day. It will go better with Christians than with others, to put it mildly (Matthew 25:46).

To illustrate this point, the modern combine is perhaps even more graphic than anything in ancient agriculture. I am completely at a loss to understand how such a massive, mighty, munching machine can get that corn off the cob without smashing the kernels. It is amazing how the corn comes through whole in spite of that violence. In spite of the violence Christians suffer in this world, the grinding pressure of tribulation, God will bring us through whole—and holy for Jesus' sake (Acts 14:22; John 16:33). In fact, He will bring us through it all in glory, brighter far than the golden grain (Matthew 13:43).

But the non-Christians, those who have not repented of their sins and have not believed in Jesus, are like the weeds, the stalks, the husks, even like the cobs that have been so closely associated with the kernels of grain. They are separated from the grain. They are meshed and mashed and mulched. They are ground into the ground again. A yet more dire doom awaits the impenitent!

What should we say? What should we do? What we should do is to say what needs to be said. Harvest time is a good time to preach—and to hear—about judgment and the end of the world. It is no accident that the church year provides for just such proclamation at harvest time. It is time to remember and to remind others about the Second Coming of Christ, His coming to judge the quick and the dead. It is time to hear and to preach the Law. Through the Law the Holy Spirit brings people to repent, to acknowledge their sins.

Then it is time to preach the Gospel, the good news of forgiveness, life, and salvation, free for sinners, costly for Christ. It has been earned and won for us by the incarnate Son of God, Who lived the life we should have lived and died the death we should have died—because of our sins. He did that all for us all (2 Corinthians 5:14-21). It is His will that repentance for sin and forgiveness for sin for His sake be preached throughout the world to the end of the world—for the salvation of sinners (Luke 24:47; Matthew 28:19-20).

POWER VERSUS SPEED

A man I know collects vehicles. He has tractors, trucks, and sports cars. He must be a man of broad tastes. Sports cars and tractors are so different from one another that the category "vehicle" hardly covers both.

"Tractor" means "puller" in Latin. A tractor is geared for power, not for speed. It pulls heavy farm implements. A sports car is geared for speed. On the road a sports car would make a tractor look as if it were standing still. In the field a tractor would leave the sports car literally standing still, unable to make it over the rough terrain.

Which is better—power or speed? To some extent that depends on whether one wants to win the Indianapolis 500 or plow the back forty. But in the long run, power counts more than speed. The world could get along quite nicely without sports cars or race cars. But life would be much harder without tractors and bulldozers. And in the long run, slow and steady wins the race, too.

Power and speed come face to face on the football field. The speedy runners and receivers get much more glamour and glory than the plodding linemen. But a football game is won or lost "in the pits," where the offensive and defensive lines clash. The fleet-of-foot types would never score a point without the hulking giants. "Three yards and a cloud of dust" was the motto of one college team. The greatest running back would hardly gain a yard if he only had other men his size blocking for him.

In high school I witnessed a wrestling match between a big guy and a little guy. The gym teacher "wanted to see what would happen." The one was wiry and quick; the other, strong and slow. The little guy was all over the big guy, but he could not move him. As soon as the big guy got any kind of a grip on the little guy, the match was over.

Jesus spoke of a strong man being overcome by a stronger one (Luke 11:21-22). Jesus was saying that His power to cast out demons is sure proof that He is stronger than Satan. That is great comfort for Christians at all times of temptation and tribulation. Our Savior is Almighty God!

Earnest pastors and active laymen are often tried by certain doubts. Why do people resist and reject the Word of God? Why do more people care more about anything worldly than about everything spiritual? Why do people rebel against a faithful pastor who is proclaiming the Word of God? That is rebellion against God (Luke 10:16)! Why does God put up with that? Satan's power is limited. God's power is unlimited. Is Satan working harder than God?

That is the question. God is infinitely stronger than Satan. So when Satan seems to be coming out on top, it seems to us that he is trying harder than God. He is not working harder than God. *But Satan is working more furiously than God.* He has to. He knows that he is outmatched in the power department. His only hope, his last hope, his desperate (that is, hopeless) hope is in furious speed. Satan's hope will be disappointed. Our hope in Christ will be fulfilled and realized for Jesus' sake.

In Luke 18:1-8, Jesus encouraged perseverance in prayer despite seeming delays in God's help. He said: "And shall not God avenge His own elect, which cry day and night unto Him, though He bear long with them? I tell you that He will avenge them speedily" (vv. 7-8). The Bible seldom speaks of speed in God's actions. It does so here in a curious paradox. God will endure with us while we suffer, but He will also rescue and avenge us quickly (see Psalms 31:2; 69:17; 79:8; 102:2; 143:7).

The usual lists of God's attributes include power but not speed. Speed is temporal, and God is outside of time. But He knows the right time for everything He plans to do. He plans to help us in every trouble. He will help us in the right way at the right time. God wants us to trust Him in spite of Satan, in the face of the foe's furious ferocity.

"If God be for us, who can be against us? He That spared not His own Son, but delivered Him up for us all, how shall He not with Him also freely give us all things?" (Romans 8:31-32; see vv. 28-39). Because Christ died for our sins, God is gracious to us and directs all things for our benefit and blessing. In His Word, God invites and moves us to trust Him for this world and the next. Based on the promises of God in His Word for Jesus' sake, that faith will be fulfilled; that hope will happen; that trust will come true.

GOD'S BOOK

Almost every American home has a Bible. Sometimes it is on the coffee table. Sometimes it is on the shelf. Sometimes the people do not know where their Bible is. As a pastor visiting in a home, I would rather see a well-worn Bible than a well-kept Bible. The Bible is to be read regularly, not just dusted occasionally.

Do you read your Bible? Do you know what it is? If you know what it is, and Whose book it is, you have a real reason to read it. Not reading it is leaving a treasure unopened and unused.

The Bible is not just another book. It is "the Book." "Bible" means literally "Book." The Bible is the Book, the best and greatest Book. It is God's Book.

God inspired the Bible (2 Timothy 3:16). He called men to be prophets (Old Testament) and apostles (New Testament). He taught them what to say and what words to say it with (1 Corinthians 2:13). That is why the Bible is God's Word, God's Book.

It was men who put pen to paper, but God is the Author of the Bible. He has authored no other book. The Word of God through the prophets and apostles is the foundation on which the faith and life of the Christian is to be built (Ephesians 2:20). It is through the Word of God that people are brought to faith in Christ (Romans 10:17).

The principle is "Scripture alone," *sola Scriptura*. Only the Bible has authority for Christian faith and life: not reason, not emotion, not tradition, not organization, not supposed new revelation. History is full of attempts to set up some authority beside the Bible. That always becomes an authority over the Bible. But Christ's disciples are to stay with Christ's Word (John 8:32). The sheep hear the Shepherd's voice (John 10:2-5).

Because God is the Author of the Bible, everything it says is true. True means not false. Not false means not in error, not erring. That is what Christians mean when they say that the Bible is inerrant. We are simply saying that it is completely and totally true. The Bible is inerrant because its Author is infallible. His Word is truth (John 17:17). That is why Jesus said, "The

Scripture cannot be broken" (John 10:35).

Everything the Bible says is true. God knows all about history, science, geography, and everything else. He created the world and everything in it. What He says about anything is certainly right and correct. So what His Book says on any topic is certainly right and correct. This is the Christian attitude toward the Bible. This is the attitude of Christ and the apostles in the New Testament toward the Old Testament.

It is important to know that what the Bible says on any topic is true. But our purpose is not merely knowledge. We are not talking about some philosophical opinion. The Bible is a practical book, with practical truth and practical wisdom.

It is important to know that the Bible is true because it is important to trust the truth, value, and wisdom of what it teaches. When someone casts doubt on anything the Bible says, he casts doubt on everything the Bible says. What it says is important for the right relationship to God. We can hardly claim to have a good relationship to a person if we doubt, distrust, and deny his words. We can hardly have a good relationship to God without listening to what He says.

God's Word of Law constantly shows us our sin. That is not pleasant, but it is necessary. We have to know about the problem to care about the solution. God's Word of Gospel constantly reassures the one who admits his sin that all his sins are forgiven because Jesus Christ, the eternal Son of God, died in place of all, for the sins of all. That is the central message of the Bible. That is the central truth and trust of the Christian faith. That is worth hearing regularly in a church where the Word is purely preached. That is worth reading in God's Book.

The Bible is God's Book. God means to bless and save us through His Word, by which He brings people to faith in Christ (2 Timothy 3:15). That should move us to read it. The Christian's flesh is still weak and makes it seem a chore to read the Bible. But the Christian's spirit wants to read and learn and be drawn closer to Jesus in true faith.

THE CHOSEN WITNESSES

Who are Jesus' witnesses? Some people say that all Christians are Jesus' witnesses. That is not the Biblical way of speaking, as a look at some Bible passages using the word "witness" (Greek: *martus*) will show.

Some people say that Acts 1:8 means that all Christians are Jesus' witnesses. That is just not so. Jesus spoke those words only to the apostles ("unto them," v. 7). The promise in those verses related directly to Pentecost. The apostles are Jesus' witnesses all over the world to the end of the world. We carry and spread the testimony. But it is still *their* testimony as the chosen witnesses, authoritative testimony recorded by divine inspiration in the New Testament.

This point is underscored by the use of the word "witness" throughout the Book of Acts.

Another man was to be chosen to replace Judas as an apostle. The main criterion for nomination was that he be an actual witness of Jesus' public ministry and of His resurrection (Acts 1:21-22). Not even all the men in that small group before Pentecost were qualified. The only ones who could be considered were those who had seen and heard these things (see Acts 4:20).

Only the apostles were called witnesses on Pentecost (Acts 2:32; see v. 14). Peter so designated himself and John in Acts 3:15. The term was applied to the apostles again in Acts 5:32 (see v. 29). Acts 10:39-41 and 13:31 also make it clear that the witnesses were only certain chosen witnesses.

The Apostle Paul had not been one of Jesus' disciples during Jesus' earthly ministry. He is called a witness only with reference to what was directly revealed to him (Acts 22:15; 26:16). Paul was very much aware of the need to establish his credentials as an apostle and witness of the risen Lord (1 Corinthians 15:8-11; Galatians 1:11-24). That is why Acts three times tells of Jesus' actual appearance to Paul on the road to Damascus (Acts 9, 22, 26).

It was important for all the apostles to assert that they were eyewitnesses of Jesus' work on earth (1 Peter 5:1; 2 Peter 1:16 *(epoptai)*; John 1:14; 1 John 1:1-3). That is why Acts 1:13 lists the apostles by name (so do three Gospels: Matthew 10:2-4; Mark 3:14-19; Luke 6:13-16). And that is why Acts 1:15-26 tells of the choice of Judas' successor. Luke opens his Gospel with a reference to the apostles' status and calling as eyewitnesses *(autoptai,* Luke 1:1-2; see Hebrews 2:3).

All of those who saw the risen Lord were also eyewitnesses in a general sense (1 Corinthians 15:6; Stephen in Acts 22:20; the others mentioned in the Gospels). But the apostles were specifically chosen by God to give the public testimony to the risen Lord, as we saw in the other verses cited above. It need hardly be said that no one walking on earth today can qualify in any sense as a witness to the events of Jesus' earthly ministry. (Note that the word "witness" is used in other ways in other contexts in Scripture. But that is not the concern here.)

What does it matter? For one thing, it is important to understand the Bible throughout and to use it correctly. It is at best silly and at worst misleading to misuse a Bible verse (Acts 1:8) to try to get people to spread the Gospel. The end does not justify the means.

A crucial doctrinal point is also at stake: the *sola* in *sola Scriptura* (the "alone" in "Scripture alone"). The sole, unique authority of the Bible is at issue. The apostles have a special place in Christianity, for it was through them that God gave us the New Testament. What they say about Jesus has God's authority behind it because they are the witnesses specifically chosen by God and because God inspired their spoken and written testimony.

We must not set ourselves up as people whose testimony matters. We are to direct others to the apostles' testimony in Scripture, for it was inspired by God. We have no authorization to communicate anything in Jesus' name except the Word and witness which He caused to be written down by His chosen witnesses.

The bottom line is that no one's faith is to depend on us, on what we say, or on what we do. Their faith is to be based and built exclusively on the Word of God (1 Corinthians 1-2).

Instead of talking about ourselves being witnesses and giving testimony, we should use the words "evangelize" and "evangelism." The latter has no counterpart in the Greek New Testament but is simply a noun derived from "evangelize," which is used quite a bit in Scripture (especially in Luke and Acts as well as in some of Paul's epistles).

"Evangelize" means to bring or proclaim good news. In Greek it could be any kind of good news, depending on the context. In the preaching of the apostles, we know that it was the Gospel of Jesus

Christ. The word is also used for the preaching of Jesus and that of John the Baptist (Luke 3:18; 8:1; 20:1) and for the specific messages the angel brought to Zacharias and the shepherds (Luke 1:19; 2:10).

"Evangelize" and "evangelism" are too often used today in a sense that restricts them to private situations in which the Gospel is spoken to unbelievers. They certainly fit those situations, as the verb "evangelize" is used for Philip's private proclamation to the Ethiopian eunuch in Acts 8:35. But in the same chapter the word is used three times for the public proclamation of the Gospel (vv. 4, 12, 25). It is used more often for public than for private proclamation (Acts 13:32; 14:7, 15, 21; 15:35).

"Evangelize" and "evangelism" should be used for both public and private proclamation of the Gospel to both Christians and non-Christians. They can be used in all those cases because the Gospel is essential. It must be the same Gospel, for there is only one real, true Gospel (Galatians 1:6-9). We all need to hear that Gospel and to keep hearing it.

The phrases, "sharing Christ," "sharing faith," and "sharing our [your, my] faith" should also be avoided. Neither Christ nor faith can be shared. What can and should be shared is the Word of Christ, the Word of faith.

Christ is neither a commodity nor an experience that could be shared. He is a Person. We cannot share Him as we could share a sandwich or a meal or a stroll in the park. To speak of sharing Christ cannot effectively carry any meaning to unbelievers.

Our faith, our own trust in Christ, cannot be shared. A Christian cannot give all or part of his faith to someone else. That is part of the meaning of the Parable of the Ten Virgins (Matthew 25:1-13). The Christian faith cannot be spread as an infectious disease is spread or as one candle is lit from another. It is spread only by means of the Word of God (Romans 10:17).

It would not be improper to speak of sharing *the* faith, the objective content of the Christian faith. The word "faith" is used in that sense in Jude 3, just as Romans 10:8 speaks of "the Word of faith." Christians certainly should share the faith in the sense of communicating that content in discussions with one another and with non-Christians. But the possible misunderstandings should make us careful about this use of words.

If we want to use the word "share," we should speak of sharing the Gospel or sharing the Word of God. The Gospel and the whole Word of God (Law and Gospel, all Scripture) can be shared as we can share news or information of any kind and as we can share any book (talking about it, giving or lending copies, inviting someone to read it with us). The Word is the tool or instrument of the Holy Spirit—the Law to bring people to repentance, the Gospel to bring them to faith in Christ.

Philemon 6 is mistranslated in several modern versions so that it sounds as if Philemon were to share his faith. The word translated "sharing" is *koinoinia*. The context (see vv. 7, 14, 18-19) shows that it refers to Philemon's generous sharing of material blessings with others. That sharing proceeded, as do all Christian good works, from faith in Christ. Paul was encouraging Philemon to be equally generous with Onesimus. The word *koinoinia* is used in the sense of a sharing or a gift to refer to the well-known financial help for the poor Christians in Jerusalem (Romans 15:26; 2 Corinthians 9:13; probably also 2 Corinthians 8:4). It has the same meaning in Hebrews 13:16. The King James Version is correct in translating it "communication" in Philemon 6, but that English word is no longer used in the sense of sharing, distributing, or giving (see Galatians 6:6, where "communicate" translates the related verb *koinoneo*).

It is vitally important that we share, spread, proclaim, publish, broadcast the Gospel. This article is intended to encourage that, not to discourage it. But to do that task, we need to know exactly what the task is. A person's witness or testimony can relate only to what he has seen or heard or experienced himself. Our experience is a complete and total irrelevancy in evangelism. What matters is the objective, inspired testimony of the apostles in the New Testament—and of the prophets in the Old Testament. That is not because their experience matters but because their spoken and written testimony was inspired by the Holy Spirit, Who still works through it to call, convert, strengthen, etc.

Faith that depends on faith is merely wishful thinking. Our faith depends only on the Word of God *(sola Scriptura)*. When we speak the Word to others, we want them to believe in Jesus, too, and in the same way, so that their faith depends only on the Word of God. Neither our faith nor our testimony can be any basis for anyone's faith.

In other words, what is at stake is the real certainty and assurance of faith. We are to proclaim the whole Word of God, both Law and Gospel, but with the main emphasis on the Gospel. We know the Gospel only through the Bible, which is the inspired, inerrant, infallibly written Word of God. Only on that basis is faith established on an unshakable foundation (Ephesians 2:20; Romans 15:4; 2 Timothy 3:15-17; 1 Corinthians 2:5, in the entire context of 1 Corinthians 1-2).

THE IMPORTANCE OF THEISM

Theism is simply the belief that God exists. At one time the debate about the existence of God did not seem very important to me. In my philosophy major I encountered all the arguments pro and con. But I really thought it a waste of time.

It was a waste of time because it was an open-and-shut case. Every intelligent person believes that God exists. Is that too strong a statement? No stronger than what the Psalmist said: "The fool hath said in his heart, There is no God" (Psalm 14:1; 53:1). Those who deny God's existence may put on a show of wisdom. It is only a show.

The mere fact of God's existence is not very personal. I always wanted to move forward to more important matters, more specific truths about God. In geography, we do not have to prove the existence of the earth. We talk about its seas, continents, climates, peoples, etc. I wanted to get past the arid debate about God's existence and into the verdant pastures of God's Word.

That was fine for me. I hope it is fine for you. But a lot of people out there are atheists—or at least practical atheists. A practical atheist may say that God exists, but he lives as if God did not exist. Because he does not apply what he knows, he is no less foolish than those who say that there is no God.

Satan is no atheist. He knows very well that God exists. But he has been working very hard to get the academic world to try to do away with belief in the existence of God. He is behind both academic and popular atheism. For several centuries he has orchestrated on the academic level the denial of everything that is not physical. In the last century or so, that denial has filtered down to the popular level.

Satan is behind everything that is atheistic—every brand and version of secularism, materialism, humanism, and the theory of evolution. They are all atheistic. They could make headway only among people who were first deluded into doubting or denying the existence of God. "Atheism" means being without God. Ephesians 2:12 calls all non-Christians "atheoi," people without God. Satan always wants to separate people from the true God.

The current situation makes it necessary for us to talk about the mere fact of God's existence. The Law is necessary before the Gospel—the diagnosis before the cure, the problem before the solution. But people no longer listen even to the Law because they do not believe in the Lawgiver. I always want to hurry right to the Gospel. But today we have to spend time on the existence of God and then more time on God's authority to give the Law and His rightful concern for the Law. Only then can it make sense to speak about Christ and the Gospel.

Can the existence of God be proven? It is a shame that the question must even be asked. The existence of God cannot logically be denied.

I was driving down the highway with some Christian young people. One of them had brought along a friend who doubted the existence of God. When the talk turned to evolution, I said that there was no evidence at all for evolution. He said that there was no evidence for the existence of God. I waved my hand at all the scenery we were passing. I said, "Look around. You see nothing but evidence for the existence of God."

It really is that simple. The Epistle to the Hebrews says: "For every house is builded by some man; but He that built all things is God" (Hebrews 3:4). David says, "The heavens declare the glory of God; and the firmament showeth His handiwork" (Psalm 19:1). On that basis no one in the world should be able to deny the existence of God (Romans 1:19-20).

All the fancier arguments for the existence of God are true and valid. But some are hard to follow. In any case, most of them are simply variations on the theme: Creation must have a Creator.

William Paley compared it to a watch. If you find a watch lying on the ground, you do not suppose that those pieces of metal just happened by chance to come together as a watch. You know that someone designed and made it. But every leaf on every tree, even every cell in every leaf—not to mention the human body (Psalm 139:14)—is more complicated than a watch, more obviously the product of intelligent design. So there must be an intelligent Designer.

If you are walking in the woods and come across even as simple a structure as a log cabin, you do not suppose that the trees grew into that configuration and died. Someone built that cabin. Someone built this world. This is sometimes called "the argument from design." It is another variation on the theme: Creation must have a Creator.

"The problem of evil" is the only objection to the existence of God that must be taken seriously. If God is good and loving and all-powerful, why is there suffering? But all our problems resulted from the fall of man into sin. Without that there would be no pain or death. God made everything "very good" (Genesis 1:31). The problems are our fault.

According to Jesus' words (Luke 13:1-5), no one gets worse than he deserves. We have all deserved the worst: damnation to hell forever. In view of sin we cannot reasonably accuse God of injustice but should praise Him for His great love and mercy in Christ and trust His wisdom in all matters.

We cannot know much about God by the use of reason. We can know something of His power, glory, and wisdom. Human reason can also know something of right and wrong, something of God's will expressed in creation (conscience; Romans 2:14-15). But fallen human reason by itself cannot go beyond a few bare facts.

We know much more about God because He has spoken and has caused His Word to be written down. The Bible is God's Word. Only the Bible is reliable for going beyond the bare facts that reason can know. Reason knows the fact that God is. It cannot tell us Who God is. Only from the Bible do we learn that the true God is the Triune God: Father, Son, and Holy Ghost. Only from the Bible do we learn the true strictness of God's Law and the terrible truth about our sinful plight. Only from the Bible do we learn the Gospel, the good news of forgiveness and salvation because of the suffering and death of the Son of God, Jesus Christ, in our place.

But we must face the fact that many people today do not know even that God exists. So we have to keep talking about His existence. Only then will it make sense to talk about His Law and our sin. And only then, finally, will it make sense to talk about our Lord and Savior, Jesus Christ.

So many false teachings of our time (Marxism, evolution, etc.) are a threat to Christianity at the most basic level because they reinforce the deceit that there is no God. The most basic way, but not the only way, to combat these teachings is to proclaim the existence of God. The existence of God is not the sum of the Christian message. It is not yet the Gospel at all. But we cannot preach Law or Gospel to those who do not yet believe that God exists. We must proclaim that God is: "I AM THAT I AM" (Exodus 3:14).

SPECIFIC CHRISTIANITY

There is a modern false religion that has no name. It cannot have a name. It is no-name religion. Generic religion is pushing froth, not faith; thrill, not truth; sentiment, not substance. No-name religion denies all thoughts (especially the true ones) but affirms all feelings (especially the false ones).

Christianity is specific and has a name. It does not claim to be the best religion. It claims to be the only religion. There is only one true God, the Triune God. He has written only one book. The Bible is the only book that is the Word of God. There is only one Person Who is both true God and true Man, Jesus Christ. He is the only Savior.

Christianity is full of specifics, particulars, details. At one place in all the world, at one time in all history, in one Virgin's womb, God the Son became a Man. His life alone was perfect. He alone kept God's Law. Then on one cross, on one hill, on one day, this one Man suffered and died for the sins of all. On the third day He rose from the dead to show that He had fully paid the penalty for all our sin.

Christianity is completely exclusive. The Word about that once-and-for-all event is to be proclaimed around the world to the end of the world to save specific sinners like you and me. The only hope for anyone to be saved is that one Person, Jesus Christ. Peter said, "There is none other name under heaven given among men, whereby we must be saved" (Acts 4:22).

A Christian is not a generally religious person from a specific tradition. Christianity is not another form of some basic substance found in all religions. Christianity is unique. It can never mix or blend. The true God is a jealous God.

People say that all religions are the same. They consider the essence of religion to be law and/or emotion. There are similarities in law. Do this and don't do that. That is as far as sinful people can get in their thinking without special revelation. There are similarities in emotion. Satan can imitate and distort. He cannot create.

But the Gospel is unique to Christianity. Jesus Christ, the eternal Son of God, became a Man and suffered and died as the only God-appeasing sacrifice for the sin of the world. Those who believe in Christ (trust that their many sins, as great and grievous as they are, have been forgiven by God because of what Jesus has done and suffered on their behalf) are saved. Those who do not believe in Christ are damned.

That is tough talk. People today call it intolerance and bigotry. To many modern minds that label itself is enough to disprove Christianity. Western society has fallen for no-name religion. The dominant form of "religious" thought in our culture today is a vague, general, mushy, contentless, sentimental religiosity that is assumed to be universal. Everyone has it or can have it, with or (better) without help.

People who cannot see the justice of sentencing a murderer to death can hardly fear that God would sentence anyone to hell. People who can justify the murder of a baby can hardly fear that God would judge any religious expressions untrue, much less positively evil.

Generic, no-name religion is the idea that any and all remotely religious feelings are to be whole-heartedly approved. The only thing that cannot be tolerated is a religious thought that claims to be true. When a person says that a statement is true, he is saying that whatever contradicts it is false. Today that is the unforgivable no-no. So rank unbelievers rant and rave against any resistance to unbelieving ecumenism.

For modern America it is fine to be Muslim, Mormon, Moonie, or Methodist as long as one does not say that any other ideas are false or wrong. Everything is fine and dandy in a person's spirit if he occasionally has a small dose of anything vaguely spiritual. Can't a person pray as well at home as at church?

Everyone supposedly has a right to his own views or feelings, and no one has a right to dispute any religious claims. So nothing is false or wrong. That is nonsense. If all views are equally right, they are all equally wrong. If nothing is false, nothing is true. No-name religion is as good (as bad!) as atheism. There is no danger in worshipping a false god only if there is no true God to punish idolatry.

Marx would rejoice about this state of affairs—if anyone could rejoice in hell. Marx said that religion was an opiate. Generic religion really is only a drug. An occasional emotional fix: is all that is needed. Sermons, slogans, songs, and sayings need no specific content. So much that passes for Christianity is empty, and some churches are less specifically Christian than a bowling league.

Christians should favor the freedom of religion. We want to be free to confess Christ. That is freedom before an earthly government. Our constitution cannot guarantee freedom of religion before God.

The solution is for pastors to be clear and specific in all preaching and teaching. That includes the choice of music; the tone of worship; the content of counselling; and the nature of outreach. We preach Christ crucified. "For the wages of sin is death; but the gift of God is eternal life through Jesus Christ our Lord" (Romans 6:23).

We must preach specific Law as well as specific Gospel. A pastor must clearly condemn sin—any and all sins. Then he must direct the penitent's attention to Christ and say with John the Baptist: "Behold the Lamb of God, Which taketh away the sin of the world!" (John 1:29). A pastor must instruct people about the love and good works that the Gospel motivates. But the emphasis must be on the Gospel!

Proclaiming the Word and hoping that unbelievers will be brought to faith is not bigotry. It is love for Christ Who died for all, and love for all for whom He died. In human law, it is no more intolerant to preach Christ than to try to convince anyone of anything. Freedom of religion does not mean that we must keep silent. It means using speech instead of force. That is fine with us. The only power we have is in the Word.

The solution is also for every Christian to be sure that his church is a church, not a religion club. A religion club makes people feel warm and cuddly-or at least smug, secure, and self-satisfied—once or twice a week. A church proclaims and praises Jesus Christ as the one and only King, Lord, and Savior. His people should be serving and praising Him in all they do. That should be specifically clear in church activities. We are God's chosen priests and people to proclaim "the praises of Him Who hath called you out of darkness into His marvelous light" (1 Peter 2:9).

WHAT IS GOD?

There are only two ways people answer the question: What is God? God is either Someone or everything. God is either the Creator of the world or the world itself. The first view is theism. The other view is pantheism. Every religion teaches one or the other in some form.

Theism is true. There is one God and He is personal. He is spiritual, not material. He is not physical, has no physical substance, no parts. He is alive and active. He thinks and wills. He is unlimited and has unlimited power and knowledge. He is everywhere present. He is eternal: without beginning, without end, without change. God created the world and works in it, but He is not part of the world. God does not belong to the world. The world belongs to God.

Pantheism is false. It uses the word "god" in a completely different sense (small "g," false god). It says that god is not personal. God is everything and everything is god. God is the world and the world is god. You are god—but so are the worm, the germ, and the pebble. There are different kinds of pantheists. Some speak of vague spiritual reality in the world. Others speak only of matter. They all make the world their god.

Theism by itself is not Christianity. It is preliminary to Christianity. We must know about God before we hear His Law. We must know about His Law—and our sin—before we hear the Gospel of Jesus Christ, which is unique to Christianity. Theism is not the whole story. It is only the beginning of the story. But the story must have that beginning. That is how the Bible begins (Genesis 1-3).

Christians, Judaists, and Muslims are theists. They agree about what God is. That is why some people think that they worship the same God. But they disagree about who God is. Only Christians believe in the Trinity. Only from the Bible do we learn that God is one Being but three Persons: Father, Son, and Holy Spirit.

Judaists and Muslims know about the nature, of God. They do not know the identity of God. They know what God is but not Who God is. We want to tell them about the Triune God—not as an abstract truth but as the concrete truth about the only Savior. John 3:16 makes no sense if one does not know about the Father and the Son. No one can believe it without the Holy Spirit.

Tom and Dick agree that their town has a mayor and that he has certain powers and duties. Tom knows him personally, but Dick does not. Tom tells Dick about the mayor and helps him get to know him. So a Christian tells a non-Christian theist about the true God.

Harry denies that any individual alone holds the office of mayor. He says that everyone is the mayor and the mayor is everyone. The town's administration happens without anyone in charge. Harry has a lot more to learn than Dick. Tom must show him first what the mayor is. Only then can he tell Harry who the mayor is. So a Christian shows a pantheist first what God is. Only then can he tell him Who God is.

Pantheists are far removed from reality. We have to start on a very basic level with them. If god is everything and everything is god, how can we talk about the difference between good and evil, right and wrong? How can—why should—anyone care about the life of the individual person if God is not personal? The pantheist must "go with the flow" of this world. There is no other option. Only a theist can believe that there is Someone strong and real outside the world to require and enable him to swim upstream in the world.

Pantheism is not limited to Asia, the birthplace of Hinduism and Buddhism. Pantheism has influenced Europe and America through philosophers such as Hegel, Marx, and Darwin; cults such as Christian Science and Hare Krishna; and entertainers such as the Beatles and Shirley MacLaine.

Christianity is exclusive: one who does not worship the true God is an unbeliever (John 5:23). Islam is exclusive: one who does not worship Allah is an infidel. But in pantheism, anything goes because everything is divine. A pantheist can be a polytheist, worshipping any number of limited gods (Hinduism). A pantheist can be an atheist, seeming to worship no god (Buddhism).

Some cults are theistic (Jehovah's Witnesses). Many cults are pantheistic (Christian Science, Hare Krishna). Mormonism is materialistic pantheism, teaching that matter is eternal. Mormons believe in many limited, temporal, material gods.

Atheism is pantheistic. It claims to have no god. But this world is all an atheist can fear, love, or trust. Atheism is the logical result of pantheism (Ockham's Razor). Pantheism does not always sound like atheism. But it is, for its "god" is nothing more than this world.

Communism is pantheistic. It bows down to the totalitarian state ("There is no god but government, and Marx and Lenin are its prophets"). Its impersonal idea of "history" directing all events to an ultimate "dictatorship of the proletariat" corresponds very neatly to other pantheistic ideas of "salvation."

Evolution is pantheistic. Theism believes that God created the world. Evolution believes that the world has developed and is still developing according to internal principles of its own. Evolution makes the world its own creator, its own god ("In the beginning, bang..."). Some people may sincerely believe "theistic evolution," but that is a contradiction in terms.

Theological liberalism is pantheistic. A clear example of pantheism in Christian guise is Paul Tillich (god as the "ground of all being"). Higher criticism is pantheistic: if this world is god, the Bible can be the product of worldly development and still be divine in origin. Moral relativism is pantheistic: it makes no sharp distinction between good and evil. Ecumenism is pantheistic: if everything is god, there is no room for exclusive claims to truth.

Pantheists are out of touch with reality, not knowing even that there is one true God, much less caring about the right relationship to Him. Pantheism makes it harder to proclaim Law and Gospel clearly because it denies the basic, natural knowledge of God. It is against what anyone anywhere at any time can clearly know about the existence and power of the Creator (Psalm 19:1; Romans 1:19-20; Hebrews 3:4).

Theism is important but it is only preliminary to proclaiming the Gospel of Jesus Christ. Mere theism knows nothing of God's grace in Christ, the forgiveness of sins because Jesus, the eternal Son of God, died for our sin in our place. We want to proclaim the Gospel for the salvation of souls for whom Jesus died.

THE AGE OLD NEW AGE MOVEMENT

What is the oldest religion in the world? Christianity is the oldest religion, for its origin is in God's eternal plan (Ephesians 1:4; 2 Timothy 1:9). But what is the oldest religion *in the world*? Which religion was in the world first?

Christianity is as old as Genesis 3:15, when God through the Gospel brought Adam and Eve to faith in the promised Savior. But in a sense the New Age Movement is even older. It goes back to Genesis 3:5, when Satan deceitfully promised that Adam and Eve would be "as gods." The basic temptation of the New Age Movement is man's idolatrous desire to be God. The "new age" it promises is already here. It is "this present evil world" (Galatians 1:4).

The teaching of the New Age Movement is fairly simple. It is hard for Christians to understand only because it is so totally different from what the Bible teaches. It seems complicated because there are so many facets and forms, so many versions and varieties of it, with a multitude of teachers and organizations pushing it. It seems like a trackless forest with dense and tangled underbrush. But the basics are simple.

The New Age Movement is pantheism, the old teaching that god (small "g"!) is everything and everything is god. It is the old lie behind Hinduism and Buddhism. It has been in the East for many centuries and has occasionally cropped up in the West. It has been coming on strong for two or three hundred years in Western civilization. It is behind supposedly Christian liberalism. It is the idea behind moral relativism (if everything is god, everything is good). It is also behind Ecumenism and Globalism (one world religion, one world government).

Pantheism is directly opposed to Christianity, to the truth about God and man. It is so exactly contrary to the Bible's teaching that a more complete contradiction can hardly be imagined. Whenever we affirm Christian truth, we deny pantheism.

For pantheism, everything is god and god is everything. We should not capitalize "god" in the pantheist sense because the word has no personal meaning. For pantheism, god is a thing, an "it." For the pantheist, god is not outside the world but in the world as the soul is in the body. This fictitious god is the soul of the world, a spiritual but impersonal concept of "nature." Everything is both material and spiritual. Everything is somewhat divine, a little bit of god. The rock, the tree, the bug, the man are all little outcroppings of this god.

Pantheism teaches the transmigration of souls (popularly called "reincarnation"). The idea is that when the body dies, the soul joins up with a new body. Successive transmigrations should mean upward mobility (cosmic yuppies?) until the soul is finally reabsorbed into god like a drop of water into the ocean. Personal identity ceases.

Nothing could be more contrary to the Bible. The Bible teaches: God made the world and is not part of it; God is personal, in fact, tri-personal (there is only one God, but the Father, the Son, and the Holy Spirit are each true God); the soul of the human individual goes to heaven or hell when the body dies and will be reunited with that same body in the resurrection.

Pantheism teaches works righteousness. For whether the next trans-migration is a step up or a step down depends on works. Various forms of pantheism disagree about the details, about which works work. But like all religions of human or demonic origin, pantheism is a religion of law alone, teaching only human works righteousness. Only Christianity is the religion of Christ's righteousness, given to us by God through the Gospel of God's grace in Christ, received through God-given faith.

Only in Christianity are we told to hope not because of what we have done—rather in spite of what we have done (sin!). We hope because of what Someone Else has done for us. Jesus Christ, God and Man in one Person, lived the perfect life and died the perfect death. He kept the laws we have broken and suffered and died in our place for our breaking them. For His sake alone we have forgiveness, life, and salvation.

The New Age Movement is preposterous. It is foolish, stupid, and silly. But that does not mean that it will not be popular. For fallen man is spiritually foolish, stupid, and silly. Fallen man is prone to fall for things like the New Age Movement, as the long history of pantheism shows.

We are surrounded by the New Age Movement. It fits with everything that does not fit with Christianity. It loves evolution (the impersonal development of this world, with no Creator outside). It pushes moral relativism (if god is developing in everything, everything must be morally good in some way). It embraces Communism (impersonal, evolutionary development in economics). It rejects as bigotry every claim to speak the real truth or to know the one true God, for it wants to make truth subjective and to deny any real religious differences.

In our preaching and teaching, we must warn our people against the New Age Movement. But that does not mean that we must become experts in this field. We should know it well enough that we can warn people specifically. But every time we teach Biblical truth, we are opposing the New Age Movement. And every Biblical truth we teach is against the New Age Movement. So our most important study, as always, remains the Word of God.

We have a fight on our hands. We need the Sword of the Spirit in our hands (Ephesians 6:17).

THE SHEPHERD

A pastor is in an awkward position. "Pastor" means "shepherd." The Bible talks about men being called by God to be shepherds of Christ's flock on earth (Ephesians 4:11; Acts 20:28). Jesus told Peter to feed His sheep and lambs (John 21:15-17). Peter later wrote to other Christian preachers, "Feed the flock of God which is among you" (1 Peter 5:2-3).

Jesus is the Good Shepherd. Some mere men are also shepherds, pastors by the will of Christ, to feed and lead Christ's flock. When mere mortal men are called shepherds or pastors, it must be remembered that Jesus is "the chief Shepherd" (1 Peter 5:4).

What is awkward about being a pastor? While a pastor is a shepherd under Christ's authority, he must also admit that he is only a sinful, fallible human being like any other Christian. He may feel "sheepish" about that, for he is also one of the sheep, one of Christ's little lambs.

It is sometimes uncomfortable to be both sheep and shepherd. When Dad and Mom leave big brother in charge, big brother is still only one of the children. He has no authority to do anything but what his parents told him to do. He is accountable to them and to his brothers and sisters.

Would it not be better if Christ were here in His physical presence? Would it not be better for Jesus Himself to preach, teach, counsel, guide, and instruct? Or would it not be better for God to send angels from heaven to lead and direct churches? It may seem to us that it would be better for Jesus Himself to preach or at least to send an angel to preach. But God knows better. God is wiser than we are. God has chosen to have sinful men do the preaching and teaching, the feeding and leading.

There is one way in which it seems better to have a human, not an angelic, preacher. An angel could only say: "You are sinners. But Christ died for you to forgive your sins." A man can say: "We are sinners. But Christ died for us to forgive our sins."

Jesus knows best. The chief Shepherd knows—for reasons that we may not know in this life—that it is better for Him to do His work as Shepherd of the Christian church indirectly through the persons of weak, fragile, sinful men. That is His choice. That is His will. But that does not mean that Jesus is not the Shepherd of His flock.

Jesus is the Good Shepherd Who gave His life for the sheep. He died for our sins in our place. Jesus is the Good Shepherd Who knows and loves the sheep. He makes us His own. Jesus is the Good Shepherd Who chooses and calls the sheep. Jesus said, "My sheep hear My voice, and I know them, and they follow Me; and I give unto them eternal life, and they shall never perish, neither shall any man pluck them out of My hand" (John 10:27-28).

Jesus is still the Good Shepherd after His ascension into heaven. He has not given up that work. He does His work as Shepherd through His Word. That means that a pastor's work, as a subsidiary shepherd, is simply to present God's Word, Christ's Word, to people.

A pastor must know that Word. So he must study that Word. He must proclaim that Word publicly and privately. He must call to repentance and to faith. And he must unmask wolves in sheep's clothing, that is, false prophets, of whom Christ tells us to beware (Matthew 7:15).

The keynote of a pastor's work must be the same as the keynote of Christ's preaching. That is Law and Gospel. That is summed up in the words of the prophet Isaiah: "All we like sheep have gone astray; we have turned every one to his own way; and the LORD hath laid on Him [Jesus Christ] the iniquity of us all" (Isaiah 53:6).

Through His Word, Jesus preserves His people in the one true faith. Through His Word, Jesus again and again calls us and brings us to repent of our sins, for we remain sinners in this life. Through His Word, Jesus again and again assures us of full and free forgiveness of all our sins because of His death on the cross in our place. Jesus gives that assurance through His Word by itself or with the water in Baptism, or with His body and blood in the Lord's Supper.

Through His Word, Jesus keeps His people together in local communions of believers. Through His Word, Jesus calls and brings yet more people to repent of their sins and to believe the good news of forgiveness, life, and salvation for Jesus' sake, and so to be members of His body and of a local communion of believers in Christ. Having finished the work of redemption for which He walked on earth, Jesus still works in human hearts through His Word.

HE MUST INCREASE

"He [Jesus Christ] must increase, but I [John the Baptist] must decrease" (John 3:30).

If ever a preacher was in a position to be tempted by pride, that preacher was John the Baptist. Crowds came from all over to hear him preach and to be baptized by him.

If ever a preacher was in a position to be tempted by jealousy, that preacher was John the Baptist. Jesus, Whom John had baptized, began to attract more people so that it was said, "All men come to Him" (John 3:26).

Pastors are tempted by pride. They are tempted to think that the church is about them, about their abilities, talents, personality, intelligence, charm, etc. The pastor is, after all, the man on the scene. He is the one who is visibly doing so much work. Even the humblest pastor, who takes the blame when things go wrong, is therefore also tempted to take the credit when things go right.

Pastors are tempted by jealousy. They are tempted to be jealous of other pastors who are more popular or more successful in human eyes. A pastor might even be jealous of Christ if he sees that some people may be more interested in the Word of Christ than in the brilliance of the pastor, or if someone corrects the pastor on the basis of the Bible.

Pride and jealousy are sins. But they are sins for which Christ died, for which He earned forgiveness. Jesus died for all human sin.

Pride and jealousy are not to dominate us. God's power in the good news of forgiveness for Jesus' sake moves us to fear and love God so that we may be humble, content with our position under Christ's benevolent authority. Pastor and people stand together under Christ's authority. More important, they stand together under the grace of Jesus Christ, which saves us.

John the Baptist is a good example of the right attitude for us pastors. Christ must increase, but we must decrease. The pastor is not to be concerned with his own personal popularity. He is not to have a following of his own. The pastor is to be concerned that he does as John the Baptist did. John the Baptist directed people to Christ, saying, "Behold the Lamb of God, Which taketh away the sin of the world" (John 1:29). John told them, "He that believeth on the Son hath everlasting life" (John 3:36).

The pastor must point people to Christ, whether he enjoys the popularity which John had at one time, or whether he gets the axe as John did later. Every other idea about the ministry is nonsense. Amen.

HOW BAPTISM SAVES

1 Peter 3:21 says, "Baptism doth also now save us." Friends of mine heard a Baptist preacher speak on that text. He devoted the whole sermon to trying to prove that Baptism does not save us. But it is neither safe nor right to go against God's Word.

Many Baptists clearly assert the exclusive authority of God's Word, the Bible. Why do they reject what the Bible says on Baptism? I am afraid that the problem has to do with salvation by grace alone through faith alone.

We are saved by grace through faith (Ephesians 2:1-10). Grace is the opposite of anger. Our sin justly deserves God's anger and our punishment. But because Jesus Christ, the Son of God, died on the cross for all human sin and fully paid the penalty due, God forgives our sin. God is no longer angry with the believer in Christ. That is God's grace in Christ. Faith receives forgiveness. It does not earn it. It does not appease God's anger. It trusts God's Word of forgiveness for Jesus' sake.

The grace is an accomplished fact because of Christ, Who said, "It is finished" (John 19:30). It is brought to us and given to us by God the Holy Spirit through the Gospel, which includes Absolution, Baptism, and Communion. These are the means of grace, the means of giving. Faith is the means of receiving. God gives the faith that receives grace and forgiveness.

Why more than one means of grace? Would it not be enough just to hear about forgiveness in the sermon or to read about it in the Bible? Why should we have Baptism and Communion? God wants to show us His love and grace in various ways.

Even human love finds different forms of expression. Friends, parents, children, husbands, and wives express their love by saying and doing different things. We find that very reassuring in human relationships. God wants to assure and reassure us about His love and grace and forgiveness in Christ. He does so in more ways than one.

The meaning and significance of Baptism and Communion are not different from the Gospel by itself. They are simply various ways in which the Gospel is expressed to assure and reassure us.

The Baptists see Baptism (and Communion) as human work.

They practice Baptism in a legalistic way, only out of obedience to Christ. Baptists baptize only because of the command of Christ. Lutherans baptize because of the command but especially because of the promise of Christ to bless us through that means.

Because they see Baptism as a human work, Baptists naturally think that when Lutherans stress the importance of Baptism for salvation, we are preaching works righteousness. But Baptism is not our work. Baptism is God's work. Baptism is not us doing anything. Baptism is God doing and giving everything. Christ does the cleansing (Ephesians 5:26).

In and through Baptism, we are born again to the life of faith. Since when does a child beget himself? Being born and being born again are the same in that respect. Neither is by the will, choice, or decision of the person being born (John 1:13).

The irony is that many Baptists preach a version of works righteousness by making faith a human work instead of God's work in us (John 6:29). That is their most dangerous error. Many Baptists assert salvation by faith alone in a way that contradicts salvation by grace alone. They make faith a good work that makes God gracious. True faith is pure and simple trust that God is already gracious for Jesus' sake.

How can any Christian deny the wonderful blessings God gives through Baptism? Baptism is "for the remission of sins" (Acts 2:38). Remission is forgiveness. Baptism is a means through which God applies to us individually the forgiveness earned for us all by Christ.

In Baptism, our sins and guilt are washed away (Acts 22:16). We stand before God "holy and without blemish" through "the washing of water by the Word" (Ephesians 5:26-27).

By Baptism into Christ, we share in all the blessings Jesus earned for us by His death in our place. We are spiritually resurrected to live the new life of faith in Christ, doing good works motivated by God's love in Christ (Romans 6:3-4; see 1 John 4:19).

By Baptism, we are clothed in Christ and His righteousness (Galatians 3:27).

Baptism is "the washing of regeneration." Through it, we are regenerated, born again, by the Holy Ghost. We are justified, declared not guilty of sin, because Jesus already suffered our punishment in our place. We have the sure and certain hope of eternal life (Titus 3:5-7).

We would not see the kingdom of God if we were not born again. How are we born again? We are born of water and the Spirit (John 3:3-5). How can it be wrong to speak of being born again through Baptism when our Lord speaks that way?

How do Baptists get around those passages? They confuse some passages with obscure exegetical gymnastics that deny the clear meaning of the text. They deny that other passages (John 3:5; Ephesians 5:26; and Titus 3:5) even refer to Baptism at all.

But what else can those passages be about? What else can the water and the washing be? "Baptize" is just an English form of a simple Greek word meaning "to wash" (used for other washings in Mark 7:4). Why should anyone deny that the Bible talks about Baptism without using that exact term in some verses?

Titus 3:5 must refer to Baptism. What other washing is there in Christianity? Why would Ephesians 5:26 refer to water at all except to talk about Baptism? Where else in Christianity is water applied? In John 3:5, there is nothing else to which the water could refer. Nicodemus was a Pharisee. When he came to Jesus, Jesus started right off on one of the most important things that a Pharisee needed to hear but had been resisting—Baptismal regeneration (see Luke 7:30).

Is Baptism necessary for salvation? What else can Jesus be saying in John 3:5? The Baptists are great at stressing the new birth—but they make it a human work of human effort. They make it a legal command, not a Gospel promise. When Jesus told Nicodemus and us that we need to be born again, He pointed out how that is to be done—water and the Spirit. God the Holy Spirit works through water and the Word to give us the new birth to the new life of faith in Christ. It is not water without the Word—but neither is it the Word without water.

Baptism is not *absolutely* necessary for salvation. God can give the new birth through the Word alone—but it is His gracious will to do it through Baptism, too. God can give the new birth without any means at all. That is comfort in cases of miscarriage, stillbirth, and, in tragic numbers, abortion. But except for such cases, when would Baptism be impossible? Where there is human life, there is water. Where there are babies, there is washing. Baptism should not be delayed.

There are other issues about Baptism: whether immersion is required; whether infants should be baptized. But they would be easily settled if the Baptists would only believe what has already been shown to be the Biblical teaching.

Baptism is washing, not necessarily immersing. Its purpose is "not the putting away of the filth of the flesh, but the answer of a good conscience toward God" (1 Peter 3:21). It is not dousing every square inch of a person's hide so that it will be squeaky clean. It is being assured of full and free forgiveness for Jesus' sake.

Baptism is not a human work but a divine work. It is God's doing, not man's doing. It does not require a mature, adult, human decision. It is simply God moving people to trust Him. In His grace and in His power, God can do that just as well with infants as with adults. In fact, with infants there is one less step. Being children already, they need not first be made childlike. The Baptists say that children must become like adults. Jesus said that adults must become like children (Matthew 18:1-6).

Have you been born again? Yes, through the washing of regeneration, holy Baptism! Thank God! To Him be all the credit, all the glory! Amen.

THREE LETTERS ON COMMUNION

The following three letters I wrote to a Christian woman who wrote to me objecting to the Biblical teaching about the Lord's Supper. I am giving the letters in an abbreviated and edited form, omitting peripheral matters. I hope that these letters answer some of the doubts that the Reformed commonly raise against the Biblical doctrine.

I.

Dear Mrs. N.

There are two related questions in our discussion. One is hermeneutics—which is just a fancy word for the principles of understanding the Bible. The other is the Lord's Supper itself.

I do not think we disagree on hermeneutics. Scripture does interpret Scripture. But Scripture never contradicts itself. What matters is not what you or I or anyone else thinks a passage says. What matters is what it actually says—and that is a matter of the words which the Holy Spirit chose and used.

I think it is a "red herring," a distraction from the main point, when you are concerned about the use of the word "cup." Everyone knows that the reference is to the contents of the cup. It is the same when I visit in a home and someone serves me coffee. If I am asked whether I would like another cup, I know that the offer is not to take away that piece of china and bring a different one but rather to refill the cup with more coffee. Jesus refers to the contents of the cup.

The Words of Institution are given in Matthew, Mark, Luke, and 1 Corinthians. There are slight variations in the wording. Jesus spoke in Aramaic, and the Holy Spirit inspired the various translations of His words into the Greek in which the New Testament was written. Each form in which the Words of Institution are given in the New Testament is a totally accurate and adequate translation of Jesus' original words, otherwise we would be denying the inerrancy of Scripture.

The reference to "this fruit of the vine" in Matthew 26:29 and the reference to bread in 1 Corinthians 11:26-29 do not contradict the words of Christ, "This is my body . . . This is My blood." You may be confusing the Lutheran and the Roman Catholic positions in this matter.

The Roman Catholic false doctrine, invented by philosophers in the Middle Ages, is that the bread and wine are magically changed into body and blood by the priest, even though they retain the characteristics of bread and wine. The philosophical argument for this position is exceedingly complex and need not concern us here since neither of us supports that position. But the point is that for Roman Catholics the elements are the body and blood of Christ and are not any longer bread and wine.

I keep referring to wine. I know that some groups use grape juice. But Jesus used wine. We know that because the Passover is in spring, many months after the grape harvest. There was no way to preserve grape juice except to let it ferment.

The Lutheran doctrine is that the elements remain bread and wine. They are not changed. But Christ's body and blood are also, by virtue of Jesus' divine omnipotence, really and truly present to be eaten and drunk. How is that possible? Well, how were creation, the virgin birth of Christ, the resurrection of Christ, etc., possible? The only answer is the power of God. How or in what way are Christ's body and blood present? That is not explained in Scripture. All we have is the fact that the body and blood of Christ are really present and are eaten and drunk in the Lord's Supper.

The problem that Zwingli, Calvin, etc., had was that they could not understand how the body and blood were present. So they denied that presence. Zwingli even said, "God does not propose to us unintelligible things to be believed."

Historically, this is the picture. The apostles and all early Christian writers who wrote about the Lord's Supper taught that Christ's body and blood were really present. In the Middle Ages, Roman Catholics philosophically explained away the bread and wine. Early in the Reformation, Martin Luther returned to the Biblical doctrine—without any philosophical explanations. A few years later, Zwingli (following a man named Honius, tragically followed by Calvin and company) philosophically explained away the body and blood of Christ, because the manner of their presence was beyond their understanding.

I am not saying this because I am a Lutheran. The opposite is the case. I am a Lutheran because I believe this. The importance again is that through the Lord's Supper, as through the Gospel in any pure expression of it, our Lord strengthens faith in the forgiveness of sins which He earned for us by His sacrifice on the cross. It is to preserve this comfort and assurance for Christians that I stand up for the truth of Jesus' words about His Supper.

I intend to present these arguments without any rancor or bitterness. I hope that you sense no quarrelsome attitude in my presentation. I am trying to write clearly because you asked me to write to you about this matter. I would be disloyal to Christ if I did not say "Yea and Amen" to all that He says. I trust that is your intention, too. I could earnestly wish that Zwingli and Calvin have never gained such a following for their opinions.

Let me assure you that I would never assert that a person must believe correctly about the Lord's Supper to be a Christian. Everyone who believes that his sins have been forgiven by God because of the life and death, the sacrifice and atonement, of the God-Man Jesus Christ, is a Christian. I want to proclaim the truth of God's Word for their strengthening in the faith.

II.

Dear Mrs. N.

Thank you for your letter. I will attempt to respond briefly. Please do not misunderstand my terseness. It is for the sake of clarity, not out of any lack of charity. Both are always necessary (Ephesians 4:15).

My statement about the widespread misunderstanding of our Lord's words about His Supper was made publicly. Therefore you have every right to pursue the matter. In fact, I am glad that it has come to public attention.

The justification for the statement is simply that it is true. If I said that anyone who thinks that the Bible does not prohibit murder is wrong, you would agree with me. We both see that "Thou shalt not kill" is clearly a prohibition of murder. The other statement is exactly the same. Jesus said, "This is My body." Anyone who says that it is not His body is in error. The error is by no means a matter of disagreeing with me but a matter of disagreeing with Jesus.

I could very sincerely regret that the Lord's Supper is a point of division between Christians. But that is not the fault of those who consent to Jesus' Word. It is the fault of those who depart from His Word. So it is the fault of Honius, Zwingli, Calvin, and all those who since their time have fostered the rationalistic denial of the body and blood of Christ in the Lord's Supper. Paul said that it would have to be so (1 Corinthians 11:19). The way to overcome that division is not to compromise but—speaking the truth in love—to proclaim Christ's Word to bring people to faith in it.

Again, I am quite willing to believe that you believe that the Bible is God's Word and that you believe what it says on many points. But if you do not believe what Jesus said about His Supper, that is a problem.

It is a problem of ethics and commitment—for consenting to Jesus' Word is part of being His disciple (John 8:31-32). It is a matter of sanctification and obedience—though I am more interested in the promises connected with the Lord's Supper than in mere obedience to a command. It is a matter of Christian growth since the Lord's Supper is a means by which Christ strengthens faith in Him. I deeply regret that Zwingli and Calvin have deprived so many people of the glorious comfort and reassurance of the Lord's Supper.

It is a major doctrine. The Lord's Supper is central to the New Testament. In fact, the only place the words "new testament" are put in conjunction in the New Testament is in connection with the Lord's Supper. It is our Lord's last will and testament—words spoken when He knew He was about to die. We must take it as a very serious matter.

The Lord's Supper also relates to other doctrines—and that very directly. It relates to the Person of Christ. The reason Zwingli and Calvin denied the real presence of Christ's body and blood in the Lord's Supper was that they did not believe that Jesus is omnipotent and omnipresent. Ultimately they separated Jesus from God the Son—making two separate persons out of Christ, following the error of the fifth century heretic Nestorius. I realize that I am getting into church historical matters of which you have probably not been informed.

Most importantly, Zwingli and Calvin denied that God really and truly conveys the forgiveness of sins through the Word in connection with water (Baptism) and with His body and blood (Lord's Supper). They believed that the Lord deals directly, not through means, thus overthrowing Christ's established and certain order. I fear that I am not being clear enough. Ultimately, it was doubt about the Gospel that was Zwingli's problem. I am not saying that is your problem—just want to tell you about the history of the matter. Denying that Christ had actually procured the forgiveness of sins for everyone, Zwingli and Calvin and others in various ways could not believe that all that remained was to distribute forgiveness through preaching and administering the Sacraments. They thought that there was something else for God or man to do. Thus they overthrew confidence in the Gospel.

What I believe—what Luther taught, what Lutherans have

always confessed to be the truth of God's Word—is simply this: in the Lord's Supper we do by mouth eat the body and drink the blood of Christ. We believe that what we eat and drink there are His body and blood. We believe that we also eat bread and drink wine. The bread is the body of Christ. The wine is His blood. We believe that simply because He said so. That is an end to all argumentation. How it can be, we do not know nor attempt to investigate nor explain. Since the Bible does not explain the how, we leave that up to God. Many matters in the Bible are not explained as to the how—but the facts are simply presented. We accept those facts on His authority. We refer to His unlimited power. We do not worry about further explanations.

The fact that Christ had not died when He instituted the Lord's Supper is irrelevant. Time does not matter to God. Jesus knew what He was talking about. The fact of the real presence of Christ's body and blood in the Lord's Supper is no more "confusing" than the doctrine of the Trinity. In fact, these matters are not confusing at all—as long as we accept the limitations of our human intellect and do not try to answer questions the Bible does not answer.

In no way is this a matter of my interpretation of anything. All I am saying is what Jesus said. It is His body. It is His blood. I am not interpreting it. I am simply believing what Jesus said. Roman Catholics and Reformed Christians have interpretations that interpret away one part or the other. Lutherans refrain from doing so.

I am not against exegesis. Nor do I see careful study of the Bible as a matter of unbelief. The Bible merits the most careful study. Not all passages are equally clear. By linguistic and other studies, it is good to bridge the gap in time, language, and culture that exists between us and the original addresses of the Bible.

I am glad that you are a "stickler" for detail. These matters are very important. In spite of the doctrinal difference, I am pleased to believe that you are a Christian, that you believe that your sins are forgiven because God died for them on the cross. I pray that you will always be comforted by the assurance of forgiveness for Jesus' sake—which is also my only hope. But the doctrinal difference is nevertheless very serious in the light of 1 Corinthians 11:29.

III.

Dear Mrs. N.
I fear that any further discussion of the Lord's Supper between

us would be beating a dead horse. The fact is that Jesus said, "This is My body." I affirm that it is His body. You deny it. That is the whole point. All your human argumentation cannot change the facts. I brought Luther, Zwingli, and Calvin into the discussion only for the purpose of historical perspective. I would not be a true Lutheran if I did not subscribe to the principle of *sola Scriptura,* Scripture alone, that is, only the Bible has authority in matters of faith and conscience.

I believe in the real presence of Christ's body and blood in the Lord's Supper not because Luther said it but because Jesus said it. Your argument is not with me nor with Luther but with Christ.

If I believed what I said because of my own interpretation, I would be guilty of pride. If I believed it because it is Luther's teaching, I would be guilty of idolatry. But the only thing I have been saying all along is, "Thus saith the Lord."

Only once does the Bible record the words, "Let there be light." Yet the light is still shining. Jesus said, "This is My body," only once. Yet it is still His body.

It seems to me that your correspondence in this matter proceeds from a great spiritual uneasiness on your part because you are trying hard to deny what you really recognize deep down inside, namely that Jesus' words are truth, that it is His body and blood.

I would be glad to speak with you about this matter. But I see no point in further correspondence. All I have to say is to quote Jesus' words: "This is My body."

HOW ARE YOU?

How are you? We understand that this question refers to one's physical health. It is commonly used in greetings and may be the most frequently asked question in the world.

When introduced to someone for the first time, we ask: "How do you do?" or "How are you doing?" Even "Howdy" is a form of the same question. When we study another language, one of the first things we learn is to ask: "Comment allez vous?" "Wie geht es Ihnen?" or "Como esta Usted?"

It is considered perfectly polite to ask about someone's physical health. Not to ask might seem impolite and even uncaring. But it is a personal question. Yet we seldom or never ask about someone's spiritual health. That seems too personal, too intimate. It might be considered insulting or offensive even to imply that someone might be in less than perfect spiritual condition.

It is a sign of concern to ask about someone's physical health. Why is it considered prying or judging to ask about someone's spiritual condition? We go straight to physical health in any conversation. We get to spiritual topics by the most roundabout way, if at all. Even a pastor, whose work is to care for people spiritually, senses that he must ask people first about their physical well-being and get around to spiritual matters only gradually and indirectly.

We ask about the body but not about the soul. We ask about disease but not about sin. We ask about physical pain but not about spiritual distress. We ask about the battle with bacteria but not about the struggle with Satan.

It is a prominent part of pride that politeness almost requires us to assume that everyone must be doing fine spiritually. Sinful pride wants to say; "I am such a good person that you should automatically recognize that I am doing fine in my spirit. And what business is it of yours anyway? How dare you even imply by a question that I might be having spiritual difficulties?"

Satan also has a hand in this business. He is the number one enemy of God and man. He has been known to make frontal assaults, but his main method is the sneak attack. He wants to lull us into a false sense of security by denying his spiritual reality and our spiritual problems. Genuine security is never attained by denying the reality, power, or ferocity of the enemy. We should want to know what he is all about and what he is up to.

It is just as caring, just as loving, and more important to ask about someone's spiritual condition than to ask about his physical health. It does not imply that we consider him a worse sinner than others, than ourselves. There need be no arrogance expressed or perceived in such a question. Christians should try to show love and concern by asking about spiritual life—whether it is present, whether it is flourishing.

Christians should know that they themselves have problems with sin, temptation, affliction. Everyone in this world has those problems. Christians are not spiritually perfect. They are still sinners in this life and face spiritual difficulties of many kinds.

Christians should also know that non-Christians have nothing but spiritual problems. Without Christ, they have no solution to those problems. The assumption that people who do not confess faith in Christ are in good shape spiritually is a serious mistake. It is the false idea that a person can do fine on his own or can have a good relationship to God apart from the Word of God and the faith in Christ that it produces. There is no spiritual life apart from Christ.

A congregation that will accept any person as a communicant without asking about his spiritual condition is considered warm and friendly. That is actually an uncaring attitude! A congregation that asks first about an individual's spiritual state, about whether he confesses his sin and faith in God's grace for Jesus' sake, is considered judgmental. That is actually the caring, loving attitude!

The spiritual diagnosis for all of us is God's Law, which tells us that we are sinners and warns of God's anger against sin. The solution to the problem, the cure for those who admit the disease, the way from death to life, is the Gospel of Jesus Christ. It is the good news that the Son of God became a Man to satisfy God's anger against our sin by keeping the laws we have broken and by suffering the punishment for our sins, dying on the cross for our guilt.

There is no sense talking about the solution if we do not discuss the problem. No one cares about a cure unless he is concerned about a disease. It should be considered extremely loving to ask about someone's spiritual condition as long as the questioner admits his own sinfulness and is motivated by the desire to share the message of forgiveness for Jesus' sake. That good news is how God gives spiritual life, health, and growth.

You will soon ask or be asked the question: "How are you?" When you hear it or say it, think about a spiritual dimension to the question in your life and in the other person's life. Think about sin as the problem. Think about forgiveness for Jesus' sake as the solution.

BECAUSE WE LOVE THEM

Why may others not commune with us? Why may we not commune with others? Why do faithful Lutherans permit only those united with us in confessing the faith to receive the Lord's Supper? Why do faithful Lutherans not commune with those outside our fellowship?

It is because we love them. Out of love for others we do not want to do anything harmful to them. Communing with them in their church or ours would hurt them, not help them. Our refusal seems unfriendly but is really very loving.

Communing together is a very intimate spiritual relationship (1 Corinthians 10:17). Such close fellowship should not be entered into lightly. We love our children and want them to hear the Word of God in our church. But we deny them Communion until they learn and confess the faith and are able to examine themselves (1 Corinthians 11:28). We love others and welcome them to hear the Word of God in our church. But we deny Communion to all who do not know, believe, and confess the Biblical faith our children must learn before communing.

Even if people do not understand why we deny them, they should be polite enough to respect our belief. Even a worldly association has the right to determine who may be granted the rights of membership. No one shows up at a club meeting for the first time and demands all the privileges of membership. But it is not merely our belief. It is the Lord's Word and the Lord's Supper. We are bound to respect His Word and will. We are not free to change what is His.

Modern people have forgotten the Biblical command that Christians be united in confessing the one true faith. St. Paul wrote, "Now I beseech you, brethren, by the name of our Lord Jesus Christ, that ye all speak the same thing, and that there be no divisions among you; but that ye be perfectly joined together in the same mind and in the same judgment" (1 Corinthians 1:10). The Word and teaching are God's, not ours. We are not free to depart from His Word nor to agree to any departure from it.

Love for others means wanting to correct them on the basis of the Bible for their own spiritual well-being, so that they have the wonderful assurance of salvation for Jesus' sake alone. That is the main message of God's Word. In religion, human thoughts, like human works, always make salvation unsure. Spiritual fellowship with those who have departed from the Scriptural truth would not be loving toward them because it is not good for them. It would confirm them in their error. We would be saying, "It's perfectly O.K. for you to go against God's Word."

We must not commune in other churches also because they do not administer the Lord's Supper according to Christ's will in the Words of Institution. In view of their false teachings and false practices, do they really have the Lord's Supper at all? The Reformed do not have the Supper instituted by Christ, for they publicly delete the meaning of His Word about it. The Roman Catholics do not have the Lord's Supper when they depart from its proper use and parade the bread about or reserve it on the altar.

We have the Lord's Supper in our churches. We deserve no credit for it but only thank and praise the Lord. We must not be proud but humble. The true body and blood of Christ are distributed to all who commune in a true Lutheran church. It is important for us to know to whom we are distributing it.

1 Corinthians 11:27-32 tells of the danger in receiving the Lord's Supper in an unworthy way, without believing that Christ's body and blood are there distributed with the Word for the strengthening of faith in the forgiveness of sins earned once and for all by Christ on the cross. Only those who believe what the Words of Institution say receive the spiritual blessing of the Lord's Supper. Those words involve the whole Biblical faith. The good news of forgiveness and salvation earned for us by Christ relates to all Biblical teaching (Romans 15:4; 2 Timothy 3:15-16).

The results of misusing the Lord's Supper include sickness and death—not to mention the guilt incurred by receiving it without the true faith (in place of the forgiveness received by the true faith). It is not loving to give a person something so dangerous without first having asked whether he will receive the benefit or the harm.

Some object: "We would not invite someone to our home and then refuse to feed him." The answer is: "But you would refuse to give him something that would hurt him." Communing someone not instructed in the faith would be like giving adult food to a baby. Communing someone who did not believe correctly about it would be like serving a guest something poisonous. It is for the weak in faith as well as the strong. But it is not for those without the proper faith.

Law and Gospel must be distinguished. The Lord's Supper is pure Gospel. Communion is an absolution. We cannot absolve those who do not confess their sins and confess the faith. That would be telling them that there is nothing wrong with the way they are living and believing. It would be encouraging them along the wrong path. That is hardly loving!

The pastor has responsibility. No responsible physician dispenses medicine without making the diagnosis. A pastor should not commune anyone without having learned that he confesses his sins and confesses faith in Christ, believing what Jesus says about His Supper. Only with that faith would he receive it for blessing and not for harm, for forgiveness and not for judgment.

We cannot look into another person's heart. We cannot judge what we cannot see. If a pastor had to be sure that a person had true faith, he could never commune anyone. He could never be sure that someone was not lying when he confessed. A pastor should see that the person confesses the one true faith and does not deny that confession by living without concern for God's Word and will. When a parishioner's life openly contradicts that confession, he comes under church discipline.

What about a person who claimed to hold the true faith but retained membership in a church that denied the Word of God? What if a Roman Catholic or a Baptist confessed the Biblical faith but would not give up membership in his Roman Catholic or Baptist church? He would be openly sinning against God's word and would have to be denied Communion (John 8:31-32; Romans 16:17; 1 Corinthians 1:10; etc.).

Why do we not commune others in our church? Because we love them and do not want to contribute to their being harmed by the misuse of the Gospel and the Lord's Supper. Why do we not commune with others in their churches? Because we love them and do not want to confirm them in their false beliefs. They may be Christians, but they are living dangerously.

Satan has made it very hard for us to speak this way in the modern world without seeming very unfriendly, very unloving, and very proud. We should try to make it clear that God has moved us to accept His Word in humility and not to trust our own thinking. We should try to make it clear that we love others and that our Communion practice is a matter of serious concern for them. We should point them to the clear Word of God. Only God can convince people of His Word.

NOTE 1: The Words of Institution are found in Matthew 26:26-28; Mark 14:22-24; Luke 22:19-20; and 1 Corinthians 11:23-25. The Lutheran teaching is the plain meaning of the Words of Institution. The bread we take and eat is the body of Christ. The wine we take and drink is the blood of Christ. That is so because of the Word Christ spoke when He instituted the Lord's Supper. The meaning of the Lord's Supper is in those words, namely, the forgiveness of sins because of Jesus' suffering and death in our place. All who eat and drink receive the body and blood of Christ by mouth. Only believers in Christ receive forgiveness there.

NOTE 2: The Reformed teach that the bread and wine are only symbols of Christ's body and blood. They say that the Sacrament depicts Christ's death but does not actually convey the forgiveness He earned or strengthen faith in it. It has no more meaning than a picture of the Crucifixion.

NOTE 3: The Roman Catholics teach that the bread and wine are magically turned into the body and blood of Christ. There is no more bread or wine left, even though the elements retain the outward characteristics of bread and wine. They say that the Sacrament is a human good work earning credit with God by re-sacrificing Christ. They use the bread and wine apart from Christ's command and promise when they restrict the cup to the priest alone, reserve the bread on the altar, and use the bread for a procession.

ARE WE PROUD?

"Oh, you conservative Lutherans! You think you're so smart! You think you're right and everyone else is wrong!"

Have you heard that complaint? I have heard it a few times, once or twice from unexpected sources. Is the complaint valid? Is the accusation just? It had better not be!

Luther heard that accusation. "Are you alone clever?" He denied that. He also pointed out that it would not be the first time that God had opened the mouth of an ass (Numbers 22).

The accusation arises because true Lutherans (orthodox, conservative, confessional Lutherans) say that this is true and that is false. We make assertions. Any assertion is also a negation. If anyone says that anything is true, he automatically says that the opposite is false.

We boldly confess the faith. Lutherans say in explaining each article of the Apostles' Creed: "This is most certainly true" (Luther's Small Catechism). Whatever disagrees is false. Whoever disagrees is either honestly mistaken or deliberately deceitful.

Is that pride? It had better not be! The cross of Christ is to be the Christian's only boast (Galatians 6:14). How can we tell whether it is pride on our part, pride in our intelligence, our education, our reasoning, or our tradition?

How have we come to believe, teach, and confess as we do? On what basis do we make such firm assertions? Why do we so boldly reject all that contradicts our confession of faith?

If we hold the faith because of our opinions, our feelings, our traditions, or our arguments, we are proud. Then we would have philosophy, not theology; man's word, not God's Word. If we thought that we were better or smarter than others, we would be Pharisees. We would be not only boasting in ourselves but also trusting in ourselves. That would be pride and idolatry!

The Word of God alone must be the only basis for any and all public and private proclamation. *Sola Scriptura,* Scripture alone, must be the source and standard for all that we believe, teach, and confess. There is no reason for anyone to believe what we say about sin, death, hell, and damnation, nor about the Savior, life, heaven, and salvation. All that matters is what God says. God has spoken and written. The Bible is His Word, not ours.

If the Bible does not speak clearly on any matter, then we need not know it. We should not try to explain what God has not explained. But the Bible does speak clearly on many matters. We are faithful to the Lord only if we believe, teach, and confess what He tells and teaches (John 8:31-32). We cannot change God's Word any more than we can change God's mind.

The Bible is clear about Law and Gospel: the condemnation of sin and the forgiveness of sin; the damnation that we have deserved for ourselves by sinning and the salvation that Jesus Christ, the Son of God, has deserved for us by living a perfect life and suffering and dying for our sins in our place. We must always be clear about Law and Gospel.

Are we proud? We are sinful. Pride is a constant danger for us. When we have been proud, we should confess that sin, and we should believe that Christ died for that sin, too. Pride should be combatted and eliminated with God's help, by God's power, through God's Word. We should be especially concerned that our natural tendency to pride does not enter into theology, preaching, teaching, or any aspect of the ministry of the Word.

We should not want people to be convinced that what we say is right. We should want people to be convinced that what God says is right. If Law and Gospel are our idea, then salvation is not only uncertain but also impossible. But if Law and Gospel are God's Word—and they are—then faith and salvation are certain. It does not depend on man's wisdom but on God's power (1 Corinthians 2:5).

When we speak boldly and plainly as we should, we should also make it clear that we are preaching not our word but God's Word, that we want people to trust and believe not us but God. If people object, they are objecting to God's Word. If they reject, they are rejecting Christ. If they attack, they are attacking God (Luke 10:16).

ARE WE ALOOF?

Are we aloof? Are we "standoffish"? Are we cold because we do not join non-Lutherans (including liberal, falsely so-called Lutherans) in worship and prayer, do not sit at the feet of their teachers for religions instruction, do not share Holy Communion with them?

Some people may say so, but that is a misunderstanding. Because their preachers encourage carelessness, members of other denominations find it very hard to understand why we are cautious in these areas.

We are not cold, aloof, or standoffish. We do not have a closed-door policy. We welcome anyone to attend our worship services and our Bible classes,to hear and learn the Word of God with us.

But out of obedience to God and love for people, we do insist on a confession of faith in clear Biblical truth before receiving someone into communicant membership or welcoming him as a guest at Communion. That is not at all unfriendly. It is genuine, Christian love and concern for the other's spiritual well-being. Is a doctor unfriendly because he asks about a person's physical health before he prescribes treatment? Is a teacher unfriendly because he asks about a person's previous education before he tries to teach him? Is a lawyer unfriendly because he asks about a person's legal status before he gives advice? Neither is a pastor or any Christian unfriendly when he asks about a person's spiritual condition. That is care, concern, and love. A willingness to help does no good if we cannot know when and where what help is needed.

We should be as friendly, warm, and sociable as possible in dealing with everyone, including Christians who deny some Biblical teachings. We may have very fine personal relationships with them.

But we do not join in worship with those who depart from Scripture. We do not put ourselves into the position of being taught by anyone who denies any part of what the Bible teaches. We do not commune with those who do not believe what Jesus says about the Sacrament.

That is not hatred but love—being concerned about the

spiritual well-being of others. For truth matters. The Word of God matters. We cannot treat departures from it lightly—because of the danger to souls for whom Christ died.

It is also a matter of obeying our Lord. He tells all Christians: "Beware of false prophets" (Matthew 7:15). The Bible teaches that Christians are to be in agreement with one another—on the basis of what the Bible teaches, because the Bible is God's Word. See Romans 16:17 and 1 Corinthians 1:10.

So we are always willing to talk about spiritual matters with others—with the Bible open! But we cannot join with them unless any disagreements are settled first. No two groups of any kind can unite and work together unless they are doing the same work in the same way.

A Christian congregation exists for the purpose of glorifying God and proclaiming His Word for the salvation of people. Obviously we cannot achieve that purpose by working together with those who do not proclaim His Word purely but mix in human thoughts and teachings. We cannot do that any more than we could work together with those who deny the Word of God entirely.

More important than God's commands in this matter are God's promises. Our Lord says: "If ye continue in My Word, then are ye My disciples indeed; and ye shall know the truth, and the truth shall make you free" (John 8:31-32). We want to remain steadfastly with the pure Word of God because of the blessings and benefits God gives us through it: comfort, strength, motivation, the assurance of eternal life for Jesus' sake.

Others may accuse us of pride, saying that we think we are right and have a monopoly on truth. That is not the point at all. It is not in pride but in humility that we bow before the Word of God, accepting all that it teaches, even if it goes against our human reason. The Lord says: "To this man will I look, even to him that is poor and of a contrite spirit, and trembleth at my Word" (Isaiah 66:2). It is God's Word, God's truth. We take no credit for it but give Him all the glory.

The reason some people mistakenly consider us proud is that they think Christian doctrine is simply a matter of human opinion, as if theology were mere human philosophy. If we did insist that we were always right about everything, that would be tremendous arrogance. We have trouble convincing others that we are not standing up for the correction of our conclusions and opinions. We are standing up for the clear truth of God's Word.

Any departure from the Word of God does lead to human thinking—to philosophy—in religion. And human thinking always leads away from the teaching and truth that we are saved only by and because of Jesus. Human teaching will always in some way tell us that we must save ourselves. The Bible always tells us in every way that we cannot save ourselves but that Christ has already paid the debt for our sin and earned forgiveness, life, and salvation for us by His life and death in our place.

As important as it is for our hearts to be focused on Jesus as our only Savior, that is how important it is to remain only with His Word in all spiritual matters. And that is also how important it is for us—out of love and concern for others—to want to direct their thoughts about religion only to Jesus and to His Word.

What seems to worldly-minded people to be pride, hatred, and insistence on human opinion is really humility, love, and loyalty to the divine Word. Only in this way is the sweet, clear Gospel sweetly and clearly proclaimed. We must not take credit for the humility, love, and loyalty any more than we take credit for the Word. It is all God's doing, and He deserves all the glory. The only pride here is on the part of those who do not accept God's Word.

FALSE FELLOWSHIP IS UNREAL

Those who believe in Christ cannot have any spiritual fellowship with those who do not believe in Christ. It is not only that they may not or should not have it. They cannot have it. It is not only wrong. It is unreal and impossible.

According to 2 Corinthians 6:14-16, there can be no fellowship between faith and unbelief. It is the same as light and darkness. There can be no relationship. Where the one is, the other is not.

People whose faith, belief, trust is different cannot really have joint or common worship. The most they can do is to be in physical proximity as each worships separately, even if they say the same words or sing the same song. If they do not worship the same God on the same basis, they simply are not really united in worship, whether they want to be or not.

If they act as if they were worshipping together, they are acting out a lie. They are acting as if they did have spiritual fellowship when they do not. They may themselves be deceived by the lie. But it is still a lie. It is show, illusion, pretense, hypocrisy, play-acting—nothing more.

We should not invite unbelievers to worship with us. Those who believe in falsehood cannot worship in truth. Out of Christian love we should invite them to hear the Word of God with us. Then they may worship with us as soon as they can worship with us, once God's Word has brought them to true faith in Christ. See John 4:24; 5:23.

The Christian believer approaches God in prayer and praise, worship, confession, and thanksgiving only through Jesus Christ (John 14:6). All of the above are in Jesus' name. They are based on Jesus' works, merit, and righteousness—not on our works. Our works are sin (Isaiah 64:6). Our worship and prayer are acceptable to God only for Jesus' sake.

The unbeliever, the natural man, the adherent of any humanly devised religion, cannot think of approaching God except on the basis of his own works and merit. His worship and prayer are not acceptable to God because of his sins. Only one who truly believes in Christ can offer acceptable worship and prayer. It is not that he is a better person (though his renovation has begun).

He is also a sinner. But he prays and worships in Jesus' name, not in his own name. His prayer and worship are acceptable to God because of Christ.

Those who do not believe in Christ, even if they do believe that there is only one true God, do not believe in the true God. That is what Jesus Himself says (John 5:23). God the Father wants to be known and worshipped only as the loving Father Who sent His Son to be our Savior (John 3:16).

The above clearly applies to total or complete unbelievers, those who do not believe in Christ at all. That includes all adherents of non-Christian religions as well as all professed or real atheists. It also includes all hypocrites, those who confess faith in Christ but do not have it. We cannot look into anyone's heart. We can only go by his confession. If he is a hypocrite and deceives us as to what is in his heart (love can be deceived—1 Corinthians 13:7), that is his problem, not ours. And a big problem it is. Christian preachers must clearly warn against hypocrisy.

But what about partial unbelievers, those who believe and confess part of the truth about Jesus? Are they believers or unbelievers? In other words, what about Christians who hold to false doctrine, some belief or beliefs that are contrary to the clear words of Scripture? Remember that the problem with false doctrine is not merely intellectual error but misplaced or misdirected trust. There is no excuse since Scripture is clear. False doctrine is always a problem for Christian faith itself.

True faith cannot have fellowship with false faith, even if the latter is only partially false. The Christian faith is exclusive (grace alone, faith alone, Christ alone, Scripture alone). Orthodox Christians cannot have spiritual fellowship with those whose faith in Christ is not pure but is mixed with other, misplaced trust. There are Biblical commands and prohibitions in this matter (1 Corinthians 1:10; Romans 16:17; etc.). But the reason for those directions and directives is the impossibility of spiritual fellowship between faith and unbelief.

When part of the Christian faith is mixed with unbelief in the same person, that causes tension and division within him. And it causes tension and division between him and those whose faith in Christ is pure. The tension must be resolved before there can be spiritual fellowship. It is resolved only when the Word of God, as the tool of the Holy Spirit, brings the person to pure faith in Christ. As far as it concerns us, we are looking for a clear confession of the Christian faith, for we cannot look into the heart.

We are not talking about persons who have not reached a certain degree of knowledge of the Christian faith. If that were the problem, then we could not have spiritual fellowship with our children until they had reached a certain level of Christian education. No, the problem is one of trust. We can have fellowship with Christians such as children who may not be able to express the Christian faith very well but do, as far as they are able, confess faith in Christ alone.

But we cannot have fellowship with persons who call themselves Christians and confess some or even most of the Biblical truth about Jesus—but who mix it with faith in human works. The Christian faith is faith in Christ alone—that God is gracious to us, has forgiven our sins, simply and solely for Jesus' sake, because of Jesus' holy life and death on the cross in our place.

Those who think that human works are in any way or to any extent necessary for salvation deny the essential Christian faith. That is ultimately the problem with all false doctrine (as well as being disobedience to God), the problem for all who have the Christian name but hear in their church the Word of God mixed with human thoughts and opinions. They may be Christians and trust Christ alone in spite of the false doctrine. But the false doctrine and false confession is a constant danger for their Christian faith, their trust in Christ. It is also a barrier between them and us—a barrier erected not by us but by their false prophets.

This includes in one way or another the Reformed, the Romanists, and the liberals of any denomination. The public teaching of all these groups is, in varying degrees and in varying ways, a denial of the Gospel and a return to the religion of the Law. It would be child's play for any orthodox church historian to demonstrate that point with reference to a large number of specific doctrines. It would be especially easy with reference to Baptism, Absolution, and the Lord's Supper, for on those matters all non-Lutherans deny the Gospel, deny that Christ has made sufficient atonement for all human sin.

To be brief: liberals deny the Gospel by denying its basis, namely, the Bible, the divinely inspired, inerrant Word of God, and by their legalism as seen, for example, in the so-called Social Gospel. Romanists openly teach that good works are necessary for salvation and, in the decrees of the Council of Trent, condemn anyone who teaches that we are saved by grace alone through faith alone. The Reformed also deny the Gospel either by making faith a human good work that saves us as such (faith in faith, decision theology) or by denying that Christ died for all (Calvinism) and by bringing back works righteousness by a number of subtle routes.

Lutherans are living a lie if they act as if they could have spiritual fellowship with those who deny the Gospel and the Sacraments or any part of aspect thereof. If we did so, we would not be acting out of loyalty to Christ—nor out of love for all who so desperately need to hear the pure, sweet Gospel. Lutherans who try to have fellowship with non-Lutherans or with liberals who falsely call themselves Lutherans can hardly be considered real Lutherans.

We distinguish between the false teachers and the falsely taught. The former must be more sternly rebuked; the latter, more gently corrected. The aim is always the comfort and consolation of souls for whom Christ died. The first item on the agenda must always be the proclamation of the clear Word of God to bring them to pure faith in God's grace alone for Jesus' sake alone. If they refuse, that is not the fault of the Word. It is their fault. If we do not tell them the Word of God, then we are at fault. But until they have been brought to pure faith, they cannot join us in prayer or worship. It is impossible. Christian love for them demands that we take things in this order so as not to confirm them in their partial unbelief or trust in self.

This is not a matter of pride on our part. It is humility (Isaiah 66:2). We are not proud when correcting erring Christians any more than we are proud when bringing the Word to total unbelievers. We remember ourselves and our weaknesses (Galatians 6:1), for we neither deserve nor claim any credit for being orthodox. We would not be orthodox if we did not ascribe all glory to God alone.

The Christian faith is summed up in the *sola gratia,* the *sola fide,* and the *sola Scriptura* (we are forgiven and saved only by God's grace in Christ, received only through God-given faith, known and believed only on the basis of God's Word, the Bible). Those who believe the three solas cannot have spiritual fellowship with those who deny them. The solas are exclusive. They reject every least little bit of legalism. The fact is that all non-Lutheran preachers are legalists in one way or another, and that includes all liberals who falsely have the Lutheran name. There are non-Lutheran people who truly believe in Christ in spite of their membership in congregations that deny the Gospel in some way. But out of love for them and for Christ we need to make them aware of that contradiction and that danger for their own good, safety, and benefit.

PRAYER FELLOWSHIP

Some so-called conservative Lutherans say that it is acceptable for Lutherans to pray with anyone who calls himself a Christian. We need to examine that issue again.

Christian prayer proceeds from Christian faith. Christians pray in Jesus' name, that is, in faith in Christ. What is that faith? It is faith in God's grace in Christ, the trust and belief that our sins are forgiven by God only because of Jesus' life and death for us, in our place. Apart from Christ we could not expect our prayers to be heard graciously, for we are frequent, daily sinners who have deserved only punishment (see Dr. Luther's explanation of the Fifth Petition of the Lord's Prayer in his small Catechism).

So the real basis of Christian prayer is God's grace in Christ. That is what the Christian trusts. The *sola gratia* (by grace alone) and the *sola fide* (through faith alone) go together (Ephesians 2:8-9; Romans 4:16). God's grace is known and faith is firm only on the basis of God's Word, the Bible (*sola Scriptura*, Scripture alone). Otherwise faith would rest on a human rather than a divine foundation and would be unsure.

Obviously we cannot pray with anyone who rejects the basis of prayer. If we are not praying on the same basis, we are not praying the same prayer at all. Faith and unbelief do not mix (2 Corinthians 6:14-16).

So with whom may we not pray? We may not pray with legalists, that is, with those who base their prayer and their hope of being heard on their own works, on the Law rather than the Gospel. But who is that?

Liberals deny that the Bible is the Word of God. But apart from the Bible we cannot know the Gospel (including the Sacraments). The Gospel is not something which human beings have imagined, felt, thought, or dreamt up. So whatever is not Biblical is not evangelical. Liberal legalism comes through in a number of ways and is well known.

Roman Catholics teach that good works are necessary for salvation. For them prayer is based on their own good works or on the works of the saints. In neither case is it Christian prayer.

But the Reformed are also legalists. There are two kinds of Reformed: Arminians and Calvinists. The Arminians, almost all non-Lutheran Protestants, revert to works righteousness in a number of ways in theory and practice, especially by making faith a human good work (it is not, John 6:29). They also pray on the basis of something they have done (deciding to follow Jesus or whatever) instead of on the basis of what Christ has done for them.

The Calvinists, of which there are relatively few left, are in a different situation. They say that God's grace is not for everyone but only for the elect. They say that Christ died only for the elect and that no one can know whether he is one of the elect. So they do not know whether Christ died for them, whether God is gracious to them as individuals. They also revert to legalism by looking at their own lives for the evidence of election. In both ways, they overthrow the basis of prayer, trust and confidence that God is gracious *also to me* for Jesus' sake alone.

We hope and believe and rejoice that, by God's grace, many Roman Catholics or Reformed are really praying on the basis of faith in Christ and not on the false basis that their denominations teach. But officially and confessionally, all except the true Lutherans are praying on the basis of works, not on the basis of grace. That means that they are praying like the Pharisee, not like the Publican (Luke 18:9-14).

But could the Pharisee and the Publican have prayed together? The Pharisee could have thought about praying with the Publican. He could have done so simply by feigning a little false humility. Hypocrisy becomes easier with practice. But the Publican, overwhelmed with the knowledge of his sinfulness, could not have conceived of joining the Pharisee in his prayer. He would never have prayed with the Pharisee—not out of pride but out of genuine humility. Neither can true Lutherans pray with those who deny the three principles: *sola gratia, sola fide, sola Scriptura*. Denying those principles necessarily means a return to Pharisaism, legalism.

I have sometimes joked with my congregation that true Lutherans always want to sit in the back of the church. But the fact is that true Lutherans do always want to stand back with the Publican rather than prancing forward with the Pharisee. When we speak out against false doctrine it is not because of pride but because of humility. We are simply carrying on our Savior's polemic against Pharisaism. And that is why we must deny church fellowship—including prayer fellowship—to those who hold to false doctrine and so teach others a misdirected trust, faith in self instead of Christ, faith in works instead of grace.

Suppose there are two petitions in circulation. Both request the same thing. But one gives a sound reason, and the other gives a silly reason. Those who sign the silly one might also want to sign the sound one. It would bolster their cause. But those who sign the sound one would not want to sign the silly one. It would bring their cause into disrepute.

It is the same with prayer. Those who pray on the basis of God's grace in Christ alone cannot join with those who base their prayer on human works—in whole or in part. God hears prayer offered in Jesus' name, in faith in Christ. God rejects prayer offered on the basis of our works—for our works are sin.

Let us not be afraid of the practical implications. We need not offend anyone by making a show of this matter. If invited to a non-Lutheran home for dinner, and if the host prays, we need not interrupt or leave. We say our own prayer silently. If asked to say the prayer, I offer a true Christian prayer in which I may say "us" but do not say "we." In other words, I may ask the Lord to bless all present, but I do not say "we pray." The matter can be clarified in peaceful discussion, if necessary or fruitful.

Much more can be said about the application of this principle. But it all comes down to being clear about Law and Gospel. Conservative Lutherans need to return to a proper understanding and practice in this matter.

PRAYER AND FAITH

Recently a non-Lutheran man asked me whether the amount of prayer or the number of prayers increased the probability that God would grant a specific request. Normally that would be a simple question, to be answered with a simple no. But the man's wife was present and had just been rattling on about a certain amount of a certain type of prayer making it certain that the request would be granted. The man wanted me to convince the wife of the error of her opinion.

The man knew the answer. The category of probability is irrelevant to God ("Known unto God are all His works from the beginning of the world," Acts 15:18). God knows in advance what we will need, what we will request, and how He will answer (Isaiah 65:24; Matthew 6:32).

The man's wife was confirmed in her delusion. But she is not the only one. The same idea is frequently found in non-Christians, who cannot be expected to know better, and in Christians, who should by all means know better. The idea is that if a person prays loud enough, long enough, hard enough, and often enough for a given thing, and especially if he can get enough other people to pray the same way, then he can somehow move God or force God to act according to man's will.

Thank God, I did not have to answer the question. Jesus answered it completely when He said, "But when ye pray, use not vain repetitions, as the heathen do: for they think that they shall be heard for their much speaking" (Matthew 6:7). Jesus rejects as a heathen idea the belief that more prayer or more prayers increase the likelihood of a favorable hearing. In the discussion I simply kept referring the woman to what Jesus said. She may not have been convinced in her own mind, but she could not openly argue with Jesus.

Trust in vain repetitions is a form of works righteousness. People see prayer as a good work that renders God favorable to their requests. Such legalism is the nature of all non-Christian religions. Even Christians still have that idea persisting in their flesh, their old sinful nature, which cannot think religiously except in terms of the Law.

The Christian truth is instead that Jesus' life and death (His perfect life, keeping the Law in our place; His atoning death, satisfying God's anger against our sin by suffering the punishment in our place) have already rendered God gracious and favorable to us. God the Father favorably hears prayers offered in the name of God the Son, that is, with faith in Christ. He does not automatically grant every specific request. But for Jesus' sake He gives us what we ask or something better, according to His wisdom. We do still pray, "Thy will be done."

It is directly contrary to the truth about God's power, wisdom, love, mercy, and grace in Christ to believe that the amount of time we spend in prayer or the number of times we repeat a specific request will move God to do what we want instead of what He knows is best. It is directly contrary to the Gospel to believe that our prayer turns away God's anger and causes Him to be gracious to us. That could only have been done by Christ, and it has already been done by Christ.

Some people will say that this position downgrades prayer. The truth is that it exalts prayer. For the briefest whisper or the merest thought in Jesus' name, in faith that God is gracious for Jesus' sake, is equivalent to thousands of hours of eloquent pleading by each of a million believers. The substance of prayer is not the way in which requests are expressed but the faith that trusts God to be gracious for Jesus' sake. Repetitions in prayer may even indicate anxiety instead of confidence, doubt instead of faith. Even worse, they may indicate faith in prayer (our work) instead of faith in God's grace in Christ. That would not be praying in Jesus' name, no matter how often Jesus' name was mentioned in the prayer.

Prayer does not change things. God changes things. Prayer only asks God to act. God acts according to His wisdom, love, mercy, and grace in Christ. There is no such thing as "the power of prayer." The power is God's power ("Thine is the . . . power"). His power is good news for us because of Jesus.

That is why Jesus can say that God will bear long with us but will also answer us speedily (Luke 18:7-8). A parishioner once told me, "God is never late." He will do what is right and best for us at the time that is right and best for us. So while we never give up on prayer (1 Thessalonians 4:17), we also do not imagine that vain repetitions will manipulate God or pull God's strings. God has no strings—and if He did, we could not pull them.

This truth does not disparage prayer. It encourages true Christian prayer, with faith in Christ, not faith in prayer. The point is not that we should pray less. We should not. But the point is that we should not believe that the intensity or frequency of a specific request will make a difference. Jesus has already made the difference by suffering and dying for our sins in our place. God the Father is gracious because of what God the Son has done and suffered in our place—not because of our prayer.

Prayer does not make God gracious. True Christian prayer is based on the faith that God is already gracious to us for Jesus' sake. That is praying in Jesus' name. Whether I get on my knees and sweat for an hour over a certain need, or whether I sit back and sigh and say, "Thy will be done," it is the same prayer, provided that it is based on the Gospel, the good news of God's grace in Christ.

The proper view of prayer is important for the Christian faith, for proclaiming and preserving the truth and the trust that God is gracious to us only for Jesus' sake. Because of Jesus we may, should, can, and do address God in prayer. Because of Jesus God hears our prayers graciously and favorably. Because of Jesus God does what is right and best for us according to His wisdom, love, mercy, and grace in Christ.

AN EMPHASIS ON WORKS

Since Luther's day, people have accused Lutherans of de-emphasizing good works. If we do not have to do good works to go to heaven, who will do good works? Why should anyone do good works? Since Luther's day, Lutherans have answered that we are simply putting good works into the right place—as the result, not the cause of salvation. Salvation by Christ alone, apart from our works, is the only motivation for true good works.

The accusation is not an attack on Lutheranism. It is an attack on the Bible and Christianity. For Lutheranism is simply Biblical Christianity. The accusation is an attack on Jesus Christ, for it denies that He is the Savior. It makes us our own saviors and our own gods, trusting ourselves to climb up to heaven by our own efforts. It is idolatry.

The Gospel is that Jesus Christ, true God and true Man, kept the Law of God perfectly for us and then suffered and died on the cross for our sins in our place. He did the job perfectly, as He said, "It is finished" (John 19:30). We are saved by God's grace alone—only because Jesus has appeased God's anger against our sin (grace is the opposite of anger). We are saved through the Gospel (expressed also in Baptism and Communion). The Gospel brings us the blessings Christ earned for us. It creates and preserves the faith (trust) that alone receives forgiveness, life, and salvation for Christ's sake.

Salvation is entirely apart from our works. The Bible says that in many ways throughout. Paul says it in so many words (Romans 3:19-4:8; Ephesians 2:8-9). Anyone who teaches that good works are necessary for salvation is opposed to the Bible and the Gospel, to Christ and God, to the prophets and apostles, and to the true Church at all times. For all Christians trust Christ alone for salvation, not themselves or their works (Galatians 5:4).

Who will do good works? Those who believe that they have been saved without works will do good works. They alone will do true good works, for they alone have the true motivation for good works. Full and free salvation by Christ alone is that unique motivation. Christ died for us so that we would live for Him (2

Corinthians 5:15).

If we did good works to earn our way to heaven, they would not be good works. They might be outwardly good, but they would be inwardly selfish. We would be loving and helping ourselves, not other people. We would be using others to get something for ourselves.

1 John 4:19 says it all: "We love Him, because He first loved us." The context explains that love starts with God loving us. Our love is motivated by God's love for us in Christ. It is God's work that we begin to love Him and our neighbor, grow in that love, and do good works that proceed from love. God should be praised and glorified for our good works (Matthew 5:16). But He will still be pleased to commend us for them (Matthew 25:31-40; 1 Corinthians 4:5).

The Bible says that God loves us first and we love Him in return. The works-for-salvation teaching says that we have to love God first and He will love us in return. But God's love is never "in return," always "in the first place." Our love is in return for His love in Christ—by His power, not our own; to His glory, not our own; for our neighbor's benefit, not our own.

That is clear in the Bible, but the fallen mind reverses it. To keep it straight, remember that good works do not result in salvation. Salvation results in good works! When we recite Ephesians 2:8-9, we should include verse 10. We are saved by grace through faith, not by or through works. But we are God's workmanship, made anew in Christ, to do good works.

Preaching that we must save ourselves by good works cannot produce a single selfless work of love. At most, it can promote outward works from inward selfishness. Preaching that we are saved by Christ alone produces real good works. God's love in Christ is not only the example but also the motivation. The Gospel is God's power to bring us not only to faith but also to love. It moves us to love God, to be grateful to God, and to want to serve God. That means wanting to serve others, whom God also loves, for whom Christ also died—that is, all our neighbors.

It is pretty hard to hate another person if we remember that God loves him just as God loves us and that Christ died for him just as Christ died for us. That is how the Gospel moves us to love and serve not only God but also man. That is how true good works are produced.

A proper emphasis on good works still means putting the main and major emphasis on Christ and His love and works for us.

HOW TO LOVE

How can I love God? How can I love God with all my heart, mind, soul, and being? How can I love God at all? How can I begin to love God? On my own I cannot love God. Cracking the whip of "Thou shalt love" condemns me as a non-lover, as a hater. It does not turn me into a lover of God.

The answer is the Gospel. God turns me into a lover by loving me and telling me that He loves me. The Bible says, "We love Him, because He first loved us" (1 John 4:19). God the Father loved me so much that He gave His only-begotten Son to be my Savior. God the Son loved me so much that He came to suffer and to die for me, for my sins, in my place.

God loves you just as much. But each of us needs to say "me" and "my" in personal faith. Jesus loves me. Jesus died for my sins. God has forgiven me for Jesus' sake.

We do not make ourselves lovers any more than we make ourselves believers. God the Holy Spirit does both through the Gospel, the message of God's love and grace in Christ. After convicting us of our sin by the Law, the Holy Spirit convinces us of forgiveness by the Gospel. The Word of the Gospel is His tool to assure and reassure us that God is no longer mad at us for our sins but is pleased with us because His Son took the guilt of our sins upon Himself and bore the punishment for our sins in our place on the cross.

The Holy Spirit makes us believers. He turns us to trust that God really has loved us so much that He went to the cross for our salvation. The same message that moves us to believe and trust moves us also to love. Once one believes the Gospel and so knows something of God's great love for him, the question is no longer: How can I love God? The question, in ever new astonishment, is: How can I not love God Who loves me so much?

How can I love my neighbor? How can I love my enemy? How can I love all other people as I love myself? How can I want what is best for them? How can I begin to love others? On my own I cannot love others. Cracking the whip of "Thou shalt love" condemns me as a non-lover, as a hater. It does not turn me into a lover of other people.

The answer is the Gospel. God turns me into a lover by telling me of His love for me and for all people. If I am aware of God's love for me in Christ—and of God's love for you and for him and for her and for them in Christ—it becomes rather harder to hate, easier to love. If I look at another person—any other person—and say to myself: God loves him the same as He loves me, and Jesus loved him enough to die for him as well as for me; it is hard to stay angry, to bear a grudge, to go on hating.

Only believers in Christ have this motivation to love. But for them it is a powerful motivation. For them to go on hating, they would positively have to resist the Gospel. They would fall from faith and grace.

But it is not simple. It is not easy. It is not a one time cure. One who has been brought to faith still struggles with doubt. One who has been brought to love still struggles with hate. We Christians are flesh and spirit, old man and new man. The old Adam is a hater. Flesh hates. Spirit loves. The old sinful nature does not love. The new spiritual nature does not hate. We have that conflict throughout our Christian lives in this world. So our love, even as our faith, must be renewed and rebuilt and rejuvenated by repeated contact with the Gospel of Jesus Christ.

In heaven there will be no more hate, no more struggle with hate. Then and there we will love God and the neighbor as we ought. That will be a big part of the joy of heaven.

GOD'S FAITHFULNESS

The "Once Saved, Always Saved" doctrine is alive and kicking. It is a false teaching about perseverance. Those who hold it say that a person who has faith in Christ cannot lose faith. Using "saved" to mean "converted," they teach that a converted person can never fall away.

It is no use confronting these teachers with people who have stopped going to church or stopped confessing faith in Christ. Since we cannot look into another person's heart, they will insist that such people either never believed or still believe.

But "Once Saved, Always Saved" is against the Bible. The Bible says that people can fall away and have fallen away. David fell away and did not repent until Nathan preached to him (2 Samuel 11:1-12:13). In 1 Corinthians 10, Paul lists other Old Testament examples and makes this application: "Wherefore let him that thinketh he standeth take heed lest he fall" (v. 12). Jesus talks about those "which for a while believe, and in time of temptation fall away" (Luke 8:13). (See Isaiah 1:2; Matthew 10:22; 24:13; Romans 11:20-21; Galatians 5:4; 1 Timothy 1:19-20).

The Bible clearly says that a believer can fall from faith in Christ. So what do we tell a troubled Christian who asks: "How can I be sure that I will not fall away?" We tell him the Gospel, the message of God's grace in Christ, the forgiveness of sins because God the Son died in His place.

The passages about falling away are not meant for troubled Christians. They are for people who are proud and secure in a fleshly way, trusting themselves not to fall away. They are for people like Peter, who bragged and boasted that he would not deny the Lord (Mark 14:29-30).

The Bible has unlimited assurance for those who trust Christ, not themselves. We go on from 1 Corinthians 10:12 to verse 13: "God is faithful." The point is to trust God's faithfulness, not our faith. Christian faith is faith in Christ, not faith in faith. If we trusted our faith, we would be trusting ourselves. That would be idolatry. It would also be foolishness, for we are terribly, fatally weak. On our own we can fall but we cannot fly. To rise, we must be raised. We must be held and lifted by God. He does that through His Word.

We are weak, but Christ is almighty. No one can take His sheep away from Him (John 10:27-30). The passages about falling away teach us not to trust ourselves. The passages about being held by God move us to trust Him more and more. See Romans 8:28-39; 1 Corinthians 1:8; Philippians 1:6; 1 Thessalonians 5:24; 2 Thessalonians 3:3; 2 Timothy 1:9-14; 1 Peter 1:5; 5:10.

By our own power we cannot begin to believe nor continue to believe. We cannot come to Christ nor stay with Christ by our own thought or effort. Through the Gospel God has brought us to Christ and keeps us with Christ. Jesus accepts us for His own sake, because our sins have been forgiven by His sacrifice for our sins in our place. Jesus will not reject us nor let go of us (John 6:37, 44; 10:27-30; Matthew 11:28).

A father carries a little child across a busy street. The mighty machines roar around. The little one's arms are clenched around the big man's neck. But that is not safety. Safety is the father's powerful arms holding the child firmly and securely. Security is not our weak hand holding on to Jesus. Security is His almighty hand holding on to us. He will not let us go.

Then why do some fall away? We do not know. We do not know why some are saved and others are lost. The Bible does not explain. We must be content to do without an answer to that question in this world.

If a person is converted, preserved, and saved, God did it. God alone gets the credit. If a person never believes or falls away, it is his own fault. Man alone gets the blame. But God wants everyone saved (1 Timothy 2:4). We do not understand. We do not have to understand. God understands.

But how about you and me? Is our salvation certain? The only answer is the Gospel, the good news of salvation for Jesus' sake. By the Gospel, God assures us of salvation. Salvation is certain because it is all God's doing.

The Biblical teaching assures and reassures us. The teaching that we can fall is a needed warning not to trust ourselves. The teaching that God holds us is the needed comfort that leads, moves, and draws us to trust Him more and more. God's faithfulness is our security. He will not change His Word. He will not forget His promises. He will not reject nor abandon His children. He will deliver us from this present evil world full of tears and take us to be with Him in heaven—because of Jesus.

WHOM DO YOU TRUST?

Recently I got a chain letter in my mailbox at a college where I am teaching a course. It threatened me with death if I did not mail out twenty copies. There is a large waste-basket near the mailboxes. That is where such garbage belongs.

Before I threw it away, I mentioned it to another professor who was there. I laughingly threw it away and told her that I was not afraid to die. She said that she was also unafraid, for she figured that she had done enough good in her life.

What an opening! She had expressed trust in her works to get her to heaven. I tried to tell her about faith in Christ and His works and His sufferings in our place. She remembered that I was a pastor. Then she said something to the effect that she had accepted Jesus as her Lord and Savior, so she was O.K. She had all the bases covered.

What did she mean? When reminded of death, her first thought was not of Christ but of her own works. When reminded of Christ, her first thought was still of what she had done, not of what He had done. Maybe she was a Christian and simply did not know how to express Christian faith. Maybe she trusted Jesus but had not learned how to say that.

But there is much room for concern that she is not a Christian. According to her words, she is at least in great danger of being in or slipping into law religion, not Gospel religion.

Many preachers preach and many people believe that we must by our own reason or strength, by our own thought or effort, come to Jesus, believe in Him, and be born again on our own. For them, "Believe in Jesus" becomes the greatest commandment of the Law, not a Gospel invitation. It becomes a demand that we must meet and fulfill. It calls for an act of our will and our power.

In reality, "Believe in Jesus" is not a command at all. It is an invitation. The Gospel is God's Word with God's power to raise the spiritually dead. The Gospel does not call for our power unto salvation. We have none! The Gospel is God's power unto salvation (Romans 1:16).

Christians believe in Jesus the same way Lazarus walked out of the tomb (John 11:43-44). Expecting someone to believe in

Jesus by his own power is like expecting Lazarus to raise himself from the dead. For the natural man is not merely sick with sin but dead in trespasses and sins, needing not to recuperate by some power within himself but to be made alive spiritually by God's power (Ephesians 2:1-10; 1 Corinthians 2:14). Lazarus walked out of the tomb—but only after God's power through His Word had raised him from physical death. We believe in Jesus—but only after God's power through His Word has raised us from spiritual death.

There was no time to go through all that with the other professor on that occasion. I only had time to say something brief to the effect that it was not that we accepted Jesus but that He accepted us, having suffered and died in our place to forgive our sins. If I have another opportunity, I would like to ask her plainly, "Whom do you trust? Jesus or yourself?"

HOW SHALL THEY BELIEVE?

The question pops up again and again. What about people who never had the opportunity to hear the Gospel? Must they be lost, damned? Is there no possibility for them to be saved? In America we usually hear that question asked about native Americans before the Gospel reached the western hemisphere. It might just as well be asked about almost any people at some time. What about the Ninevites before Jonah, the Indians before Thomas, the Germans before Boniface?

Can a person be saved without having heard the Gospel? Paul says it all in Romans 10: "For whosoever shall call upon the name of the Lord shall be saved. How then shall they call on Him in Whom they have not believed? And how shall they believe in Him of Whom they have not heard? And how shall they hear without a preacher?" (Romans 10:13-14; see Joel 2:32).

If we ask more questions in this area, we quickly get into matters which are beyond our understanding (Romans 11:33). The whole matter must be left up to the will of God. We must not, dare not, accuse God of being unfair to those who died without having heard the Gospel. We cannot know why God did not provide more intense preaching for Tyre and Sidon, Sodom and Gomorrah (Matthew 11:21-24). We still know that He wants everyone to be saved (1 Timothy 2:4). We must leave it at that.

Some people have tried to say that such people could have believed without having heard. That is contrary not only to Romans 10 but also to the whole discussion in the first two chapters of 1 Corinthians. There is no faith in Christ apart from the Gospel of Christ (Romans 10:17; 1 Peter 1:23-25). We should remember that the Word in general has gone out to the whole world—if not the Gospel, then the Law, so that there is no excuse for sin (Psalm 19:1-4; Romans 2:1-15; 10:18). We should also remember that at two different times, everyone in the world was a Christian—right after God converted Adam and Eve, and when only Noah's family was left alive on earth. There has been a great deal of Christian missionary work, stretching far and wide, especially at the time of the Apostles and as a result of the Reformation.

All attempts to say that there is salvation apart from the Gospel must end up in works righteousness. It is usually phrased in such a way that one doubts (by human reason!) the damnation of non-Christians who were "good" people. That was true when Zwingli, one of the fathers of the Reformed, said that he expected to see Socrates and Plato and others in heaven. It is true when modern Romanists try to claim that "good" non-Christians are "anonymous Christians." The idea is that salvation comes to people because they are good, not because Christ was good for us and in our place—keeping the laws we have broken and dying for our breaking them. The only hope for salvation is hope in Christ—specifically and by name (Acts 4:12).

Biblically, we have no reason to expect to see anyone in heaven except those who have been brought to and kept in faith in Christ by means of Word and Sacrament, the Gospel by itself and in connection with the water in Baptism and the elements in Communion.

We really ought to stop asking about those already dead. It is not a practical question. It has nothing to do with our task in mission work. We can do nothing to help those already dead. We have no responsibility for them. What is practical is that we still today have the requirement, the duty, the task, the labor, the joy of preaching the Gospel to all people now alive! There is nothing more urgent than spreading the Word of God. For there is no other way for people to be saved than by Christ through the Gospel. That is the point of Romans 10 and many other sections in the Bible.

It is a waste of time and energy to think about our ancestors in Africa or America, Asia or Europe, before missionaries reached them. But it is important and urgent that we spend our time and energy bringing the Word of God, Law and Gospel, to those alive in this world today and preserving the Gospel for future generations (if there are such before Christ returns). We cannot do or accomplish anything toward this goal on our own. But Christ can do everything through the Word which He wants us to spread and proclaim.

THANK GOD, WE ARE CHRISTIANS

Some time ago a news item said that, according to a pastor, a well-known convict had "found Jesus" in prison. It occurred to me that Jesus was not the one who had been lost. We should hope that the convict was brought to faith in Christ. We should also hope that he gave God the glory for his conversion instead of taking credit for it himself.

Years ago an evangelistic campaign used the slogan, "I found it." Buttons and bumper stickers were distributed with those words. Someone asked me whether it should not be, "I found Him." I suggested that it should be, "He found me."

It is amazing to hear those who profess faith in Christ speak as if a person converted himself, as if a person could by his own choice and effort, make himself a believer in Christ. The Bible says clearly that fallen man cannot do anything at all toward his conversion, much less convert himself (1 Corinthians 2:14).

The Apostle Paul never once, in all his letters to Christians, thanks them for believing in Christ. But he regularly thanks God for their faith in Christ (Romans 1:8; 1 Corinthians 1:4-6; Ephesians 1:15-16; Philippians 1:3-6; Colossians 1:3-6; 1 Thessalonians 1:2-5; 2 Thessalonians 1:3-5; 2:13; 2 Timothy 1:3-5; Philemon 4-6). He gives God alone all the credit, all the glory and gratitude, for their faith.

Christianity is completely different from human religions. Every human religion teaches that we must try to get to God by our own efforts. The Bible teaches that God has come to us in His grace and power. Every human religion is a feeble failure. Christianity is a supreme success.

There is no ladder by which we sinners can climb to heaven—and if there were, we would not have the will nor the strength to climb it. But God has come to us, to save us, to rescue us, to take us to Himself in heaven.

God the Father sent God the Son to become a true Man, to live as we should have lived, to die as we should have died—all in our place, to earn for us the forgiveness of all our sins: God the Father and God the Son have sent God the Holy Spirit to work in us through Word and Sacrament—to bring us to the faith and to keep us in the faith. God-given faith receives the forgiveness and salvation that Jesus earned for us.

In John 1:41, Andrew says that they had "found" Christ. He means that they knew where Christ was located, for He had come to them. Jesus is everywhere (Ephesians 4:10). We "find" the Lord only where He comes to us: in the Word and the Sacraments (Isaiah 55:6-12).

HOW DO YOU SPELL FAITH?

In Walther's day, a seminary student once had to repeat part of his education because he had trouble spelling. He had a problem with orthography, not orthodoxy. But many people get into theological difficulty because they misspell the simple word "faith."

Many people think and speak as if they spelled the word "faith" with a capital "I" in the middle, overshadowing the rest. They see faith as an achievement of the human ego deciding to believe and trust. They make faith in some sense a good work that accomplishes or contributes something toward salvation.

Faith is not a human work, a human product. Faith is God's work (John 6:29). It has to be God's work because we cannot even begin to do anything toward it on our own (1 Corinthians 2:14). Faith must be based on God's power, not man's wisdom (1 Corinthians 2:5).

If we produced our own faith, faith would be silly. We would be trusting and believing ourselves instead of God. That would be idolatry. If we convinced ourselves to believe that our sins were forgiven, faith would not be standing on solid ground. It would only be wishful thinking.

If someone has been mad at you and you want to know that he has forgiven you, you must hear it from him. It is no good merely to imagine that he has forgiven you. He must tell you, show you, convince you. If we are to be convinced that God has forgiven our sins, we must be convinced by God. God does convince, assure, and reassure us through the Gospel in Word and Sacrament. That directs our attention not to ourselves but to Christ.

The Law directs our attention to ourselves. It tells us what sinners we have been. It shows how we have deserved eternal damnation by offending God in thought, word, and deed. But the Gospel, the good news of Jesus Christ, directs our attention away from ourselves and to Christ alone.

John 3:16 should be read in context. Read John 3:14-15 and compare that with Numbers 21. The Israelites who were bitten by the fiery serpents died if they looked within themselves for the resources to fight off the venom. When they looked outside themselves, to the brass serpent on the pole, they lived. If we sinners look within ourselves for anything to contribute to our salvation, we die. Our constant gaze should be directed to Christ and His cross, where He, the sinless Son of God, suffered and died in our place to pay for our sins.

Christian faith is faith in Christ! It is not faith in ourselves. It is not faith in faith. It is faith in Christ alone. Faith receives the gift of forgiveness, life, and salvation for Christ's sake alone. Faith does not earn nor accomplish anything for our salvation. It does not even go out and get it. The gift is delivered by God the Holy Spirit through Word and Sacrament. Then good works result from salvation.

But do not I believe? Yes, I believe. I do the believing in the same way in which Lazarus did the walking when he came out of the tomb (John 11). He walked out of the tomb, but he had not raised himself from death. The Christian believes in Christ, but the Christian has not raised himself from spiritual death to the life of faith. Jesus gave Lazarus life through His Word. Jesus has given us life through His Word (Ephesians 2:1-10).

How should we spell "faith"? We should spell it with a very small, humble, contrite "i" kneeling at the foot of the next letter—the cross! The cross should be written large. The cross of Christ is what matters. The cross of Christ is what has made the difference.

Christianity emphasizes Christ crucified (1 Corinthians 2:2). Liberalism emphasizes God the Father. Charismaticism emphasizes God the Holy Spirit. Both also emphasize man. But the Father wants to be known as the One Who loved us so much that He gave His Son for our salvation (John 3:16; Romans 8:32). The Spirit wants to be known as the One Who testifies to the Son and glorifies Him (John 15:26; 16:14).

Christianity emphasizes Christ. For Jesus is not merely God and not merely Man. He is both God and Man in one Person. We are saved purely and only because of God incarnate. The only Man we trust, glorify, and worship is the Man Who is God, Who died for our sins and rose again—Jesus Christ alone!

THE UNFREE WILL

A man approached me and expressed the desire to join the church. We soon made plans for his instruction in the faith. It went well until we got to the Third Article of the Apostles' Creed. He balked at Luther's explanation that we cannot believe in Christ by our own thought or effort but have been called to faith by the Holy Spirit through the Gospel.

The man, who later confessed the faith, objected first that his conversion to Christianity, and specifically his desire to join our church, had happened on his initiative. I am sure it seemed that way to him. But things are not always as they seem. Most people believe that fallen man has spiritual free will. They believe that honestly, but they are honestly mistaken.

The Bible clearly teaches that fallen man does not have spiritual free will. On his own, fallen man can only think and plan evil (Genesis 6:5; 8:21). We are born sinners and are unable to help, change, or save ourselves (Ephesians 2:2-3; Psalm 51:5; John 3:6; Romans 2:3; 7:8). Fallen man is by nature blind, dead, and an enemy of God (Psalm 14:3; Romans 8:7; 1 Corinthians 1:21; 2:14; Ephesians 2:1-3; 4:18).

Many preachers say that people are "sin-sick." That phrase is popular because it is alliterative and sounds good. But it is inaccurate unless one would speak very graphically about a total, terminal illness (Isaiah 1:5-6). For our natural sinfulness is not disease but death. We were dead in trespasses and sins until God quickened us, made us alive in Christ, through water and the Word (Ephesians 2:1-10; Titus 3:5-7; John 3:5-6).

In Bible class, someone asked whether Jesus said anything to this effect. First I made the point that whatever the prophets and apostles said by the inspiration of the Holy Ghost is just as much the Word of Christ as are the words that our Lord spoke while He walked on earth (John 16:12-15). But then I showed that Jesus had said this exact same thing about conversion.

Jesus said that our believing in Him is the work of God (John 6:29). No one can come to Him in faith without being drawn by the Father (John 6:44). Some people rejected this and other statements by our Lord and went away (John 6:60). Jesus did not turn on the charm or the super salesmanship. He kept speaking the same truth, that coming to Christ in faith is a gift of God (John 6:65). More disciples became former disciples (John 6:66). Jesus asked the apostles whether they would also leave. Peter said, "Lord, to whom shall we go? Thou hast the words of eternal life" (John 6:68).

Why insist on this truth? Can a person not be a Christian without knowing these facts? Well, a person can be a Christian in spite of great ignorance. Baptized infants are good examples. But we should not remain in childish ignorance but should mature in understanding God's Word (1 Corinthians 14:20). It is tempting to say that we should not preach and teach this truth because it is difficult for people. But that would not be following Jesus' example or Jesus' command.

This controversy has at times gotten very noisy and very confused. In early nineteenth century America it led to the verse: "You can and you can't/You will and you won't/You're damned if you do/And damned if you don't." But the confusion of some people and the contradiction of others is no reason to give up the clear teaching of God's Word.

We will not understand this truth fully in this life. Here we are up against the very limits of human reason. We must stay with the Biblical teaching that God wants everyone saved (1 Timothy 2:4) but that people are converted to faith in Christ only by God's will and choice (John 6:44, 65; Romans 8:28-30; Ephesians 1:3-23; 2 Timothy 1:9). We cannot accept. We can only reject (1 Corinthians 2:14). The damned get all the blame for damnation. But God deserves all the credit, all the glory, for the salvation of the saved (Acts 13:46-48).

Those who say that they believe in Christ by their own choice cannot be very secure. How does their faith differ from wishful thinking? We should never believe anything because we choose to believe it. Today is a sunny day. I believe that not because I want to believe it but because the bright light streaming through my office window convinces me. If I am to believe that someone has forgiven me for wronging him, I must hear it from him. If we are to believe surely that God has forgiven our sins for Jesus' sake, we must be convinced by God's Word.

We believe in Jesus in the same way in which Lazarus came out of the tomb. Jesus' Word had first made Lazarus alive. (John 11:43-44). Jesus' Word of forgiveness and salvation because He died for our sins in our place has made us spiritually alive and brought us to faith in Christ (Ephesians 2:1-10; Romans 10:17).

Billy Graham once wrote a book, *How To Be Born Again*. But

which of us read a book about how to be born the first time? We are born to this life without having been consulted about it. We are born to eternal life not by our will but by God's will (John 1:13).

This truth is important for the assurance of our faith, our strengthening in believing that our sins really have been forgiven for Jesus' sake. If salvation, conversion, and perseverance depend at all on us, if it is at all up to us to start believing and to keep believing in Christ, we are lost. For we cannot do it (1 Corinthians 2:14). Christian faith is faith in Christ, not faith in ourselves. We do not keep ourselves in the faith. We are kept in the faith by God's power (1 Peter 1:5).

Our faith is uncertain if we trust ourselves to hold on to Christ. Christ teaches and tells us that our salvation is sure and certain and secure because He holds on to us (John 10:28-30). That is important not only because it is true but especially because it is comforting, strengthening, and reassuring for our faith. The idea that salvation depends on our will and our choice, comes not from the Bible but from human reason and human pride. Teaching Law and Gospel contradicts human reason and human pride. That may hurt. But it also saves.

WHAT IS TRUTH?

The philosopher Friedrich Nietzsche said that the most profound thing in the New Testament was Pilate's question, "What is truth?" (John 18:38). Nietzsche may have read the New Testament. But he neither knew nor believed its truth.

People today are very skeptical. Many ask Pilate's question: What is truth? They doubt and deny that we can know the truth. This doubt is a sort of desperate faith, a conviction that they cannot be convinced of truth. People want to justify their ignorance, their unbelief, their errors, and themselves by the hopeless hope that there is no truth, or at least no knowing the truth.

What good is a question by itself? "What is truth?" is asking, not answering. These are not even the best words we have from Pilate. Much better are the one statement we know he wrote and his firm defense of that statement.

Pilate wrote the truth when he had affixed above the dying Savior's head a placard proclaiming: "JESUS OF NAZARETH, THE KING OF THE JEWS" (John 19:19). Pilate may not have meant it correctly. But that statement is true. In fact, it is Gospel truth.

"Jesus" means "Savior" (Matthew 1:21). In fulfillment of prophecy, He was rejected by men and despised as a Nazarene (Matthew 2:23; John 1:46). He is David's Son as well as God's Son, the rightful King of the Kingdom of God (Matthew 1:1; John 1:49). He is the King Who sacrificed Himself for His people. He shall reign forever over the true Jews, all people who believe in Him and the forgiveness, life, and salvation He won for us by His suffering and dying for our sins in our place (Romans 2:28-29; Philippians 3:3).

The Jewish leaders objected to the words Pilate had written. Perhaps Pilate was tired of being pushed around. He insisted, "What I have written I have written" (John 19:22). Even a human ruler must at times insist on sticking with his words. We do not respect any man who does not stand by his word. How much more should we expect God, Who cannot err and never changes, to stick with His Word?!

Putting it in writing makes it even more binding. A man is more careful about what comes from his pen than about what comes from his mouth. Spoken words can be lost in the air. Written words stay put. That is the purpose of writing them down. Pilate was weak and pliable. But even he stood by what he had written. God is strong and immoveable. There is no doubt that He will stand by what He has written.

What God has written, God has written. God stands by His written Word. Jesus said, "The Scripture cannot be broken" (John 10:35). What God has written stands forever true. His Word will never pass away (Matthew 24:35).

God's Word is Law and Gospel. The Law tells us about our sins and God's anger. But the Gospel tells *us* about our Savior and God's grace, the forgiveness of our sins because of Christ's suffering and death in our place. The main message of God's Book is the Gospel, the good news. God arranged to have even Pilate write it and post it. Jesus died for all our sins.

What is truth? It is written!

THE HUMAN HEART

The human heart is a common symbol in modern America. It generally stands for love, most often in the romantic sense. But did you know that the main points of the Biblical message can be shown in passages that talk about the human heart?

In the Bible, the heart has nothing to do with romance. It is the seat of thought, intention, and will. The Lord says, "Out of the abundance of the heart the mouth speaketh" (Matthew 12:34). We should love God with all our heart (Matthew 22:37), that is, with all our thoughts, intentions, and purposes.

But since the fall into sin, the human heart is opposed to God. God said, "For the imagination of man's heart is evil from his youth" (Genesis 8:21). The Lord said, "For out of the heart proceed evil thoughts, murders, adulteries, fornications, thefts, false witness, blasphemies" (Matthew 15:19). Every sinful word or deed was first a sinful thought. We sin more often in thought than in any other way.

It is sad for a person to realize that his heart is sinful, but it is necessary to know the problem to be prepared for the solution, the forgiveness of sins. The psalmist wrote: "The sacrifices of God are a broken spirit: a broken and a contrite heart, O God, Thou wilt not despise" (Psalm 51:17).

The message about sin breaks the heart. But Christ heals the broken heart with the message of forgiveness that He earned for us by His perfect sacrifice on the cross in our place. Faith in Christ, the God-Man, is trust that our sins are forgiven for Jesus' sake. This faith is given to people through the Word of forgiveness. The Apostle Paul wrote: "But the Word is nigh thee, even in thy mouth and in thy heart; that is, the word of faith, which we preach; that if thou shalt confess with thy mouth the Lord Jesus, and shalt believe in thine heart that God hath raised Him from the dead, thou shalt be saved" (Romans 10:8-9).

Believing in the resurrection of Christ means believing that by raising Jesus from the dead God showed that He has accepted Christ's sacrifice and forgiven our sins. With this Word and the faith it produces, the Bible says that Christ dwells in the believer's heart (Ephesians 3:17).

This Word and faith give the believer great joy. David was inspired to write, "But I have trusted in Thy mercy; my heart shall rejoice in Thy salvation" (Psalm 13:5). Jeremiah had been told that he was to face severe persecution for preaching God's Word, but he still said, "Thy Word was unto me the joy and rejoicing of mine heart" (Jeremiah 15:16).

It may be nice to talk about the heart in a romantic way. But it is much better for all of us to think about what God says in the Bible about our hearts. Why not look up Matthew 6:19-21 and see what Jesus was talking about when He said, "For where your treasure is, there will your heart be also"?

THE OVERALL THEME

In a meeting about stewardship, someone said, "Stewardship is evangelism." So I commented, "Evangelism is stewardship." To my surprise, people not only took me seriously but even thought that I had expressed a profound new insight.

I had meant to be slightly sarcastic. If we make a word mean everything, it may eventually mean nothing. It is not helpful to emphasize one aspect of church work so that it dominates all aspects. All things ecclesiastical are related. But we need to know how they are related and how they are distinct. We cannot do everything at once, and we cannot do everything in the same way.

Stewardship is important, but it is not everything. It is one aspect of one doctrine. It is one of the most helpful and most practical ways to talk about good works. It is very closely related to the Gospel, for through the Gospel, God moves us to love Him and our neighbor and so to do good works. But it is a mistake to make stewardship central to all Christian teaching.

What is central? The overall, overarching, crucial, central, fundamental, and most basic theme of Christianity is the Gospel itself. That is the hub. Other doctrines are the spokes and the rim. They are vital. They must not be ignored. But they must be held in connection with the Gospel. All Biblical teachings are Biblical and practical only in relation to the Gospel.

Maybe I am simple-minded. I am a back-to-basics person. I believe that schools should emphasize reading, writing, and arithmetic. I believe that coaches should drill athletes in the fundamentals of their sport. I believe that Christians should always remember the basics: Law and Gospel; our sin and God's grace in Christ.

The whole Bible is Law and Gospel. Everything in the Bible is Law or Gospel.

Manfred von Richthofen, the Red Baron, was the most successful fighter pilot of World War I. He expressed his ideas about aerial combat very plainly: "Find the enemy and shoot him down. Everything else is nonsense." We should have an equally plain attitude about Christian war and work: The Law shows our sin. The Gospel shows our Savior. Everything else is nonsense.

It makes no difference whether we say that the overall theme is the Gospel or Law and Gospel. The Gospel needs the Law, and the Law serves the Gospel. The Law comes first to tell us of our need for forgiveness. The Gospel brings the forgiveness that Jesus, the Son of God, earned for us by keeping the laws we have broken and by suffering and dying in our place for our breaking God's laws. The Gospel makes us grateful to God and so moves us to love God and our neighbor. Then the Law gives direction to that love.

Whether we are talking about evangelism or stewardship, education or worship, life or death, the beginning or the end of the world, the Gospel is central. The eyes of faith must, by the Word, be kept focused on Jesus. That is true for every aspect of church work and the whole Christian life. Everything else is nonsense.

SUMMARY

The Christian faith can be expressed in few words or many words. The Bible, the book that God wrote, is a hefty volume. But it contains many short summaries of the Christian faith. Other good writings about the faith come in various sizes, from pamphlets to multi-volume works.

The summaries are short and sweet. We should want to learn all that God has told us in the Bible. That is a job for more than one lifetime. But we should not lose sight of the simple, straightforward, summary statements.

Over the years I have considered many outlines for presenting the Christian faith. Such an outline should include all the topics of the Bible. But it should be as straight and narrow as an arrow, always getting directly to the point. I keep coming back to a seven-point outline for the main topics of theology: God, World, Man, Christ, Word, Church, End.

If you can tell people what the Bible says on those seven topics, you can present the whole Christian faith, all Christian teaching. We cannot understand, define, or explain God perfectly. Much mystery remains. But the Bible speaks clearly enough for us to know about the true God and to trust Him for salvation. That is all we need to know.

Orthodox theologians have used many different outlines. That does not matter. What matters is the content. This outline could be used to present the same subject matter that Luther, Chemnitz, Walther, Pieper, and others present in various forms at various lengths.

In the Bible, God used a different outline than any of the above. In God's book, the basic arrangement is historical. The Bible records the facts of the faith in basically chronological order. Then it gives further explanations in other books. One should read first the historical books, then the prophetic books; first the Gospels, then the Epistles.

But what is missing from the outline suggested here? God, World, Man, Christ, Word, Church, End. That covers it all.

God: There is one and only one divine Being. But three

Persons are each true God: Father, Son, and Holy Ghost. God is present everywhere, knows everything, and can do anything. God is perfect. God is holy. God is just. God is loving.

World: God made the world out of nothing through His Word. That happened in six days about six thousand years ago. The world is not part of God and God is not part of the world. God made the world very good. Any problems in it are not His fault. God did not forget about the world after creating it. He governs and preserves it and blesses us in it every day.

Man: Man was made by God in the image of God. Man is body and soul/spirit. Man was created to love God totally and to love his neighbor as himself. But Adam and Eve, the parents of the whole human race, fell into sin, disobeying God. Now we are born sinful and are powerless to save ourselves. Man was created good and is still essentially good. But we are in the corrupt condition of sinfulness and commit many specific sins against God's Law (the Ten Commandments). We have deserved damnation.

Christ: God the Son became a true Man, Jesus Christ. True God and true Man, He was born of a virgin, lived a sinless life, and died on the cross for all human sin, in place of every sinner. He rose from the dead, proving that God has accepted His sacrifice and forgiven our sins. He reigns forever, and we are His forever.

Word: The Bible is the Word of God, written by God through men, and is completely true. The main teachings of the Bible are Law and Gospel. The Law proclaims God's wrath because of sin and condemns our sins. The Gospel proclaims God's grace because of Jesus and forgives our sins. The Gospel is proclaimed not only in preaching and teaching but also very significantly in Absolution, Baptism, and Communion. Through the Law, the Holy Ghost brings people to acknowledge their sinfulness and to know their need for forgiveness. Through the Gospel, the Holy Ghost brings people to trust that their sins have been forgiven for Jesus' sake. The Gospel brings all spiritual blessings: the new birth to the new life of faith; growth in faith, hope, joy, peace, etc.; and the start and growth of love for God and the neighbor (Gospel motivation, sanctification).

Church: All believers in Christ and only believers in Christ are members of Christ's body, the church. Because we cannot look into one another's hearts, the church is invisible.

Christ wants His people to be gathered locally around Word and Sacrament (Third Commandment). Through the local flock, God calls men to preach and teach, to administer the Sacraments with careful stewardship, and to exercise spiritual supervision over the flock.

End: When a human being dies, his soul/spirit goes to heaven or hell. Christ will visibly return to earth at the end of the world. He will raise all the dead and glorify all believers. Unbelievers will go to hell, body and soul, to suffer forever. Believers will go to heaven, body and soul, to praise God and to enjoy His presence forever.

That sums it up pretty well. Every Christian will see that many more specific statement are needed, especially about the Sacraments. Of course, every point would have to be proven by reference to Scripture alone. But that could all be done, and well done, with this outline.

This message is to be preached around the world to the end of the world. This message is to be preached for the salvation of the precious souls for whom Christ died. He died for all. We should want to proclaim this Word to all. That is what it is all about.

THE WORD OF HIS GRACE

Farewell Sermon
Immanuel Lutheran Church
Georgetown, Ontario, Canada
February 23, 1986

"And now, brethren, I commend you to God, and to the Word of His grace, which is able to build you up, and to give you an inheritance among all them which are sanctified" (Acts 20:32).

My dear friends in Christ! We are all aware that this is my final, my farewell sermon as pastor of Immanuel Lutheran Church. What shall we think about today? What shall we talk about now? Today we shall think and talk about what we have always thought and taught here. We shall think not primarily of ourselves but of Jesus Christ, our Lord and Savior.

If we look at ourselves, what do we see? We see sin! For we are sinners. You and I are sinful people, who have not loved and obeyed God as we ought. Nor have we loved each other as we ought. This is not just some formula that we recite, mentioning in passing that we are somewhat less than perfect. It is reality. It is the truth about us that we are very, very sinful indeed!

Sin is serious. Sin offends and angers God. And we do not want God to punish us. The punishment we are talking about is no slap on the wrist but an eternity in hell, a place of pure torment greater than any pain on earth. But if we do not want God to punish us, then we do not want Him to be angry with us. How can He not be angry with us in view of our sins? How could our sins be hidden from Him Who sees and knows all things?

Let us not move too quickly away from the subject of our sin. Sometimes I have asked myself whether my preaching here has been severe enough and specific enough about sin. Yet I personally know my great need for forgiveness, my great need to hear about the forgiveness of sins. We all need that. Talk about sin should always serve to make us more aware of that need. We need to keep the Gospel, the good news of forgiveness for Jesus' sake, as the main focus in our spiritual lives. That is why, in Christian preaching, the Gospel, not the Law, must predominate.

But it should not be thought that sin is not serious just because it is forgiven. If we offend a friend or relative, we know how hard it is to restore that relationship to its former beauty and harmony. How can we imagine that offending God is less serious, less damaging, and easier to overcome? Offending Him is more, not less, serious than offending people on earth.

In fact, our sin is so serious that the only way for it to be forgiven was for someone else to be punished in our place for all our sin. That Someone else is the Son of God Himself, Jesus Christ. And so let me keep my promise—and obey the commission of Christ to all true preachers—and concentrate on Christ, emphasize Jesus!

God is offended by our sin. The only way we can be forgiven is the way He specifies and teaches. We cannot be forgiven—saved—by our own cleverly thought-out devices, ways, means, and methods. It must be done God's way. And God's way, the only way, was the way of the cross.

God the Father loved us so much, even in spite of the atrocity of our sin, that He sent His true, eternal Son to become a Man, to live a perfect life in our place, keeping the commandments we had broken, and then to be found guilty in God's sight for all our sin, to be condemned to suffer and die on the cross for our sins.

The Prophet Isaiah says: "All we like sheep have gone astray; we have turned every one to his own way; and the LORD hath laid on Him the iniquity of us all" (Isaiah 53:6).

We are concentrating during the season of Lent on Jesus' sufferings. But Lent leads to Easter, when we will celebrate His return to life in His body, His real resurrection from the dead. Jesus paid the penalty for our sins, paid it in full. So He could not be held any longer in the punishment. He rose from the dead. He lives and reigns forever—to save us.

That is the message our text calls "the Word of His grace." It is also known as the Gospel, the good news that our salvation has been accomplished by Jesus for us and in our place. Our salvation is accomplished, for Jesus said from the cross, "It is finished" (John 19:30). We need not work and slave for forgiveness, the grace of God, and eternal life. That is rather all God's free gift—free to us, though it cost Jesus dearly.

What is "grace"? The word "grace" simply means the opposite of anger. God's anger against our sin meant hell and damnation for us. God's grace in spite of our sin, because of all that Jesus has done for us, means heaven and salvation. Our sins have been forgiven for Jesus' sake, and so God looks on us no more as sinners but as perfectly holy people—clothed in the righteousness and holiness of Christ. That is the Word of grace.

How important is the Word of grace, the message that God is no longer angry with us for Jesus' sake? Well, if you offend someone on earth and are anxious to know that person has forgiven you, how are you going to find out about his forgiveness? The only way to learn and know that he has forgiven you is for him to communicate that forgiveness, which is in his heart, to you.

So it is between us and God. To be assured that God has, in His heart, really and truly forgiven us all our sin, He must be the One to tell us that, to reveal it to us. We cannot know and be sure about it in any other way. The Word of His grace is the message that He has actually, for Jesus' sake, forgiven us all our sins. He has pardoned us. He no longer holds our sin against us.

Through this Word, the Holy Spirit of Christ assures and reassures us about forgiveness, life, and salvation—all freely given to us by God because of Jesus' life and death for us and in our place. The Holy Spirit works through this Word by itself or in connection with water in Baptism, in connection with the Body and Blood of Christ in Communion. The Holy Spirit works through this Word to bring us to faith, to keep us in the faith, and to move us to works of love that proceed from faith.

And that faith is faith in the true God, faith in Christ, faith in the forgiveness and grace of God, earned, deserved, and won for us by Jesus. It is the confident trust and belief that God actually is gracious to us, in spite of our sins, because of our Savior, Jesus Christ, "the Lamb of God, Which taketh away the sin of the world" (John 1:29). God is no longer angry with you or me, and that is only because of Jesus.

When the Apostle Paul took leave of a group of pastors in our text, he said that he commended, entrusted them to the care of God. So today let us entrust one another to the care of God, which is the only hope for any of us. But Paul said more. He got specific. For the Christian religion is specific.

St. Paul entrusted his friends to the Word of God's grace in Christ. So let us today entrust one another to the Word of God's grace in Christ. It is the chief theme of God's written Word, the Bible. It is the means by which the Holy Spirit brings to each of us the benefits and blessings won for us by Christ. And a sweet and wonderful, precious, joyous Word it is!

It is also a powerful Word. St. Paul told the friends, to whom he was saying good-bye, that it was able to build them up spiritually, to strengthen their faith, to nourish them and make their souls flourish under the grace of God. It is the tool of God the Holy Spirit to bestow these blessings.

So today we are all reminded that this Word, which, thanks to God, has been preached here for years, this Word is able to build us up also, to confirm, strengthen, establish our faith in God's grace and forgiveness for Jesus' sake.

The blessings of the Word of God's grace in Christ are infinite and unlimited. St. Paul summarizes them by saying that this Word assures us of eternal life with Christ in the glory of heaven, which is the inheritance of the saints, that is, of all whom God regards as holy and sinless for Jesus' sake. This inheritance belongs by right to Jesus Christ, the Son and therefore the heir of God the Father. But for His sake, God has adopted us as His children and heirs also. This inheritance is brought to us, assured and insured to us by His Word of grace and forgiveness.

So today we say good-bye but not a last good-bye, farewell but not a final farewell. I will no longer be your pastor, but we may see each other again as Christian friends and brethren. Many people have been talking about visiting in the future. I hope it happens. But it is uncertain whether or not that hope will be realized.

The real reason why this is not a last good-bye or final farewell is "the sweet hope of a blessed reunion in heaven." Because of that certain hope of reunion, Christians can never bid each other farewell forever. We hope to be home together in heaven. And that will be a better, happier, and more permanent home than we have ever known on earth. There will be no parting from one another—but infinitely more important, there will be no parting from our loving and beloved Savior, Jesus Christ.

Remember Jesus! Remember what the Bible says about Him! Read your Bible. Keep coming to church to hear and learn about Jesus. Through the Word, the Holy Spirit will keep us in the one true faith, faith in Jesus. Staying with the Word means staying with Jesus!

"And now, brethren, I commend you to God, and to the Word of His grace, which is able to build you up, and to give you an inheritance among all them which are sanctified." Amen.

He took upon Himself and slew it by His death. He earned for us the complete forgiveness of all our sins. He won for us the grace of God, peace with God, joy in God, and the hope of everlasting life before God's smiling face.

Because of all Jesus did and suffered for us; through the faith, hope, and trust in God worked in us by the message of Jesus, the Gospel; our fears, our tears, and our years lose their sting. They cannot deprive us of comfort, assurance, peace, and joy in the secure knowledge of eternal salvation for Jesus' sake—and of God's help along the way in ways we cannot now fully comprehend.

When we look back from the eternal maturity of glory, we will realize how silly and childish we were in this life. But we will not regret that we were like children in one way—in the comfort we were granted by our Father's hand holding ours, our Father's arms holding us—in Christ, through His Word.

BECAUSE I LIVE — AN EASTER PLAY

Characters: Cathy, Carol, Adam, and Steve are all in their early twenties. Cathy and Carol are sisters. Cathy is married to Adam; Carol, to Steve. All but Steve are faithful church members. Also a pastor (male!) who is somewhat older appears in the pulpit. Smitty is a newspaper reporter, and the Chief is his editor.

Settings: Act I takes place in the living room of the home belonging to Cathy and Adam. Acts II and IV take place in their dining room. Act ID requires a pulpit in a church and a newspaper office.

Act I

Carol is dressed as she might be for a shopping trip. She is sitting in Cathy's living room. Cathy is dressed more casually, as for relaxing around the house. Cathy enters, carrying a cup of coffee for each of them.

Cathy: Do you still take yours with cream, Carol?
Carol: Oh, of course, Cathy! Marriage hasn't changed that.
Cathy: But marriage does change a lot of things, doesn't it? Oh, listen to me talk! I don't mean to sound like an old married woman. Adam and I have only been married fifteen months.
Carol: That's still a year longer than Steve and I have been married. But even in the short time we've had, I already notice that marriage does make life a lot different.
Cathy: One difference I don't like is that we just don't get to see each other as often as we used to.
Carol: If I remember right, there were times when we both lived at home that we didn't exactly want to see so much of each other.
Cathy: But it's always going to be that way sometimes with sisters, isn't it? But after all, blood is thicker than water.

Carol: So is mayonnaise.
Cathy: (giggling): What's that supposed to mean?
Carol: I don't know. It just seemed like the thing to say.
Cathy: Really, we haven't talked that often since you got married. How is marriage? Are you and Steve getting along OK?
Carol: (defensively): Of course we are! Just like a couple of lovebirds. Why do you ask?
Cathy: I'm sorry. I didn't mean to upset you. I was just asking because I care.
Carol: I know. It's just that Mom and Dad weren't very happy with Steve when we were going together. And I know they didn't exactly like it when we first got engaged. It was a lot different from the way they acted when you and Adam got married!
Cathy: You know they love you just as much as they love me.
Carol: I know that. I love them, too. But I do have my own life to live.
Cathy: You know, Adam and I saw this movie on the late show the other night where this guy actually asked this girl's father for permission just to ask her to marry him.
Carol: When was that? The Middle Ages? (Pause.) You know, though, when I think about having kids, I guess I'll probably be just as concerned about who they marry.
Cathy: It must be sort of inevitable. I hope that we love our kids as much as our folks loved us all along.
Carol: And in our case, I don't think that they need to worry. Your Adam and my Steve are both great guys. It's just that....
Cathy: It's just what?
Carol: It's just that I wish Steve would come to church with me. I mean, we got married in that church. I feel so conspicuous sometimes, coming there without Steve. Then I see Adam there with you, and that doesn't make me feel any better. It's not that I'm sorry I married Steve. It's not that at all. I want to be his wife, as much as ever. I just wish he'd go to church, that's all.
Cathy: I didn't exactly talk this over with Mom and Dad. But I think that's the only thing they ever really had against Steve.
Carol: It didn't help, though, the first time I brought Steve home, when Dad tried to convert him on the spot. I mean, like, it was over the first cup of coffee! At least the pastor took time to get to know him before he tried to get him to come to church.

Cathy: But don't you want the same thing? Aren't you working on him, too?

Carol: Mostly, I just pray for him—a lot. And I do what the pastor said — or I try to, just to be the best wife I can be and let him see that being a Christian helps me be a better wife. (Pause) Cathy, do you and Adam ever, uh, fight?

Cathy: I guess I have to say that we have had, uh, a little unpleasantness from time to time. I suppose all couples do, at least sometimes. Why?

Carol: Oh, it's just that Steve and I have had a couple of arguments lately.

Cathy: Anything serious?

Carol: No, not exactly. I guess it's just normal to expect people to get mad sometimes.

Cathy: The important thing is that you forgive and forget!

Carol: Oh, I know that. But when Steve gets mad, he stays mad for a long time. Once he hardly said a word to me for almost two days. When I get mad, I get over it. It takes him a long time.

Cathy: Why do you think that is?

Carol: I don't know. People are just different, I guess. One time he did ask me how I could be so quick to forgive. I didn't know what to say. Finally I just told him it must be because I had always heard so much about forgiveness at home—and at church.

Cathy: When Adam and I fight, we try to talk about it after we calm down. One thing we talk about is how Jesus died on the cross to forgive us for all our sins. You know, it's pretty hard not to be forgiving when you think about Jesus.

Carol: Yeah. But see, that's something that doesn't mean anything to Steve.

Cathy: At least, not yet!

Carol: (hopefully): Yes! That's true, isn't it?

Cathy: Are you going to be coming to church on Maundy Thursday and Good Friday?

Carol: I hope so. I'm going to try. You know, Steve gets jealous sometimes, about the time I spend at church. I tell him that I'd be very happy to share that time with him—at church. But he hasn't come around yet.

Cathy: That was a hard thing for Adam and me to get used to. When we were first in love, you know, we had a hard time remembering that we were supposed to love God even more than we loved each other. It took time, but I think

we've both gotten to understand it better now.
Carol: So for now we'll keep on praying for Steve anyway.
Cathy: Say, why don't the two of you come here for dinner some evening soon. It's been weeks since we've all seen each other. How about Wednesday?
Carol: That sounds great! I'll check with Steve tonight and give you a call.

End of Act I

Act II

Adam, Cathy, Carol, and Steve are sitting around a dining room table. On the table are dessert plates, empty except for forks and crumbs, also coffee cups and perhaps a coffee pot.

Steve: Well, that was really a great meal, Cathy. You cook almost as well as your sister.
Adam: Very diplomatically put, Steve!
Cathy: We both learned our cooking in the same place, you know. And you know what it's like when Mom goes all out in the kitchen. Are you two going to be at their place for the big family dinner on Easter Sunday?
Carol: (looks at Steve): I think so.
Steve: Well, of course! I wouldn't be much of a son-in-law if I would dare risk offending my mother-in-law by not showing up—with a big appetite—when she's cooking for a family get-together. Right, Adam?
Adam: It doesn't hurt, though, that it's not hard to have a big appetite in her house. But just to make sure that we all build up a big appetite, we should all go to church together first.
Steve: There you go again!
Cathy: It's just an invitation, Steve.
Carol: Yeah. It's not like you had to bring a bulletin from church as a kind of banquet ticket or anything.
Steve: Well, maybe I will go to church. It can't hurt, I suppose. But speaking of going places, Adam, you and I need to get out a calendar and make some plans to go to a few baseball games. If I can get a day off from work, I'd like to go to one of those weekday afternoon games early in the season. I just happen to have a schedule here. (Pulls

a card out of his pocket or wallet.)

Carol: You men and your sports! Sometimes I think you almost make a religion out of that.

Steve: You girls should go to the stadium with us for a game some time. (Pause, gesture, spreading his hands apart.) It's just another invitation.

Adam: (smiles): Turnabout is fair play.

Carol: We'll talk about it—after church on Easter!

Steve: It's not that I'm against religion or anything like that, you know. It's just that I don't believe in it for myself. I don't need it. Religion is just a crutch.

Cathy: So, who's not limping?

Steve: I can stand on my own two feet!

Adam: For how long?

Steve: My mother was very religious, you know. She used to take us to church and Sunday school. But my father never went. So I figured a long time ago that religion was just for women and children. Anyway, if my Dad went to hell with all of his friends, I guess I'll be happy enough there, too. It sure won't be lonely!

Carol: (hurt): You'd be there without me!

Steve: Aw, Carol, Honey, I didn't mean it that way. You know I don't believe there is a hell anyway—or a heaven either. This life on earth is all we've got. And you know I want to spend my life here with you.

Cathy: You have to realize, Steve, even if you don't believe these things, Carol does. And we take them very seriously.

Adam: And it isn't just women and children, either, Steve. In my case, my Dad was just as faithful as my Mom. And the same is true for our in-laws, yours and mine.

Steve: I haven't been in a church yet where there weren't more women than men, though. Why is that?

Adam: I don't know. In fact, I heard our pastor asking the same question once. He didn't have any answer for it either, except he said in some cases, he thought, a man's pride got in the way. You know, the old male ego. But there are a lot of good men in churches, too. You can't deny that.

Steve: I guess not.

Adam: You see, a real church isn't about some vague, sentimental, emotional thing called "religion." It's about a Man, Jesus Christ.

Steve: Wasn't this Jesus guy just a wimp, though? I mean, the picture I always have of Him is one I guess I saw when I was a kid. There were children all around Him.

Adam: There's nothing wrong with a man who likes to be around children!
Steve: Well, I didn't mean that.
Adam: Besides, have you read the New Testament?
Steve: Not lately.
Adam: There were women as well as men who listened to Jesus when He was preaching on earth. Jesus cares about all people: men and women, all ages, all nations. But as for the idea that Jesus was a wimp, nobody ever got that impression from the Bible, I'll tell you. He talked tough when the situation called for it. And two different times he chased a bunch of crooked businessmen out of the temple all by Himself—once even using a whip.
Carol: And He had to be very brave to face all that He went through, the torture and all, being crucified. It makes me shudder just to think about it. It wasn't a pretty picture. But He did it because He loves us.
Cathy: He went through all that because we are sinners. Steve, do you know that you're a sinner?
Steve: Hey, nobody's perfect!
Cathy: It's a lot more serious than that.
Steve: Are you saying that you people are all better than me?
Cathy: No! Not for a minute. We are all sinners, too. We are not Christians because we are better than anyone else. But Christ does want to make us better people.
Steve: Don't gang up on me, all right?
Adam: Sorry if it seems that way, Steve. I think we can change the subject now. It's just that we want you to know that we do care.
Cathy: It's just that we know the blessings of Christ, and we want you to enjoy them, too.
Carol: Steve, you know that I care about you. I haven't nagged you about going to church, have I?
Steve: No. I'll say that for you. You certainly haven't.
Carol: But Honey, I know I'm going to heaven because Jesus died on the cross for all my sins. He died for your sins, too. I want you to know that. I want you to have the same thing I have—eternal life for Jesus' sake. That way we can be together forever—in heaven.
Steve: Look, I said I'll go to church on Easter. But beyond that, I'm not making any promises. We'll just have to leave it at that.

End of Act II

Act III

On camera, we see a pastor wearing vestments, standing in the pulpit. He delivers this segment of a sermon.

The text for our sermon this Easter Sunday is John 14:19. Our Lord Jesus Himself says to His disciples: "Because I live, ye shall live also." Jesus died on the cross. He died for the guilt of all human sin. We commemorated His death on Good Friday with great solemnity. But His death was by no means the end of the story. He died, but He did not stay dead! He rose from the dead and came back to life in His body. His body was glorified, that is true. But it was still the same body. The disciples recognized Him, and they still saw the wounds in His hands and side, the wounds made when He was crucified.

Jesus' resurrection from the dead is what Easter is all about. Jesus had died for our sin. He rose to show us that His death had paid for our sins in full. Death was the penalty. Death could not hold Him because He had paid the penalty in full.

Death could not hold Him. And death cannot hold us. Jesus rose from the dead Himself. And He gives us eternal life—not just that the soul goes to heaven when we die—but also that the soul and the body will be reunited when Jesus comes back. Jesus, the eternal and almighty Son of God, will raise us from the dead, too, by His power. We will live with Him in joy and glory forever—for His sake. That is most certainly true!

Insert some Easter music.

Smitty and the Chief are dressed for work around the newspaper office. Smitty is at a desk, working at a word processor. The Chief walks in with notes in hand.

Chief: You about done?
Smitty: With you in a minute. (Presses a few keys and the printer begins to work.) What can I do for you?
Chief: I want you to write up this story Jones just phoned in.
Smitty: Bad news?
Chief: Page one bad news!
Smitty: Hang on a minute. Let me make sure I can read your notes. Is this the headline: "Two Sisters Killed by Drunk Driver"?

Chief: Yeah. Then put in the subheading: Tragic End to Easter Weekend for Local Families.
Smitty: (reads): Two sisters. That must be their married names. (Shows the page to the Chief, pointing to the names.)
Chief: Right.
Smitty: (reads): Killed late in the afternoon on Easter Sunday. Just left their parent's home. On their way to a convenience store. Going to buy something for the holiday meal. Other driver hospitalized. Police say he was DUI. Can we put that in?
Chief: Jones says he's certain. Let's print it. We don't have a name for him yet.
Smitty: You want me to write up just this information?
Chief: Yeah, for now. Jones in trying to get more on it.
Smitty: That's what I hate about this job.
Chief: What's that?
Smitty: Bad news, even on Easter.

Insert some Easter Music.

We see the pastor in the pulpit again, delivering this part of the funeral sermon.

The text for this funeral sermon is the same text we considered just a few days ago on Easter Sunday. In John 14:19, our dear Lord Jesus said to His disciples: "Because I live, ye shall live also."

A Christian funeral is a very serious occasion, especially so in this case, a double funeral for these two young sisters. They are sisters to each other, but also to all of us in the congregation, for they are our sisters in Christ. We will all miss Cathy and Carol. It is a very sad thing for us to commit their bodies to the ground in Christian burial as we are doing today. It is sad because we will not have the pleasure of their company any more in this world.

But a Christian funeral also has a distinct element of joy, a joy that only Christians know. As deep as is our sorrow, especially for those who were closest to Cathy and Carol on earth, we believers in Christ still have the assurance and comfort of Christ's promises, particularly the Easter promise in our text: "Because I live, ye shall live also."

Cathy and Carol are now with their Lord Jesus, enjoying His unveiled presence in heaven. We mourn with the mourning of impatience. We do not know how long it will be until we are reunited with them. But our faith, our trust in Christ, is such that we definitely hope to be reunited with them in Christ's unending kingdom.

We bury their bodies today. But every Christian burial is a burial in hope. We have not only the hope of a reunion with them in heaven but also the very real hope of the resurrection of the dead. At the end of the world, their souls will be reunited with their bodies. They shall live again in these bodies which we bury today. And there is no death to end that eternal life.

We have this hope not because Cathy and Carol were such good people. They were sinners just as we are all still sinners in this world. But we have this hope purely and solely because of our Lord Jesus Christ, Whose death on the cross was the punishment for all their sins—and for all our sins. Jesus rose from the dead. And He will raise Cathy and Carol and all the Christian dead to live with Him in glorified bodies forever. We have this hope because He lives. And He promised, "Because I live, ye shall live also."

End of Act III

Act IV

Steve and Adam are in Adam's home, having just come from their respective jobs. They are well dressed but have loosened their ties. Steve is sitting at the table where all four had sat in Act II. Adam enters with two coffee cups.

Adam: You take yours black, right, Steve?
Steve: Right.
Adam: I don't know what the coffee is going to taste like. It's been less than a week since the girls—were killed. Not much time for me to learn to make any kind of coffee, I guess. I used to do OK in the kitchen before Cathy and I got married. At least I thought I did OK But I never made anything to her satisfaction. So I just let her handle that end of things.
(Awkward pause.)
Adam: I'm glad you dropped by Steve.
Steve: You said you wanted to see me.
Adam: I like you, Steve. I don't know if we're still considered

relatives. I'm not sure whether we ever were brothers-in-law, being married to sisters. I mean, Carol was my sister-in-law, and you were Cathy's brother-in-law. But I'm not sure whether or not that made us bothers-in-law.

Steve: I don't know either. What difference does it make?

Adam: That's right. I guess that's what I'm really trying to get at. I'd like for us to go on being friends in any case. Everybody needs friends, right?

Steve: If you say so.

Adam: It was hard, going back to work the past couple of days. I had trouble getting my bearings. I guess everybody knew about Cathy and Carol. Things were a bit strained. Most people just sort of said they were sorry to hear about it all. Then for the rest of the day they just sort of steered clear of me. I guess they just didn't really know what to say.

Steve: You mean, like you just really don't know what to say to me now?

Adam: I guess so.

Steve: But don't you miss your wife? I don't know. Maybe you weren't as happy as Carol and I were. Why, we were really just newlyweds! And then for this to happen! We had such dreams, such plans! We were going to buy a house and have a family. Now all our dreams and plans are gone forever.

Adam: Maybe the plans you had are all gone. But Carol had plans beyond this world.

Steve: Oh, I know. All those nice things the preacher said about Carol being with Jesus now. I guess if there is a God, and if there is a heaven, then Carol is certainly there. She was an awfully good person!

Adam: Did you really listen to the sermon—on Easter or at the funeral?

Steve: Yeah, I think I did.

Adam: Then you know that the preacher didn't say she was in heaven because she was good but because Jesus was good. Now I don't claim to know exactly what was in Carol's heart—or in Cathy's heart for that matter. But I know the way they both talked. They both used to say that their hope for heaven and for the resurrection to glory was based on Jesus Christ and what He earned for them.

Steve: Oh, but I don't know how all that stuff can be true!

Adam: It's not up to us necessarily to see how it can all be true. The hows and the whys we have to leave up to God. But the fact is that it is all true, that much we see in God's Word, the Bible.

Steve: I'm glad for you that you can believe all that stuff.

Adam: I can't believe it any more than you can believe it. Look, you've known me long enough to know that I'm a pretty sensible kind of guy, right?

Steve: Yeah, except for this religion business.

Adam: That, too! I've never gone in for wishful thinking. All our wishing and hoping could never bring Carol and Cathy back to life. If I thought that I had convinced myself that this religion business, as you put it, is true, then I would give up believing in it, too. But it's God who convinced me of it. He convinced me by His Word.

Steve: That's just somebody else's wishful thinking.

Adam: No. It's a matter of fact that Jesus did rise from the dead.

Steve: You can't prove that.

Adam: It's been proven. When Jesus died, the apostles, the ones He had chosen to tell the world about Him, were in hiding like a bunch of cowards. They were scared stiff. They feared for their own necks. But a few weeks later, they were already telling the world that Jesus had risen from the dead and that they were the public witnesses to prove that.

Steve: Maybe they were all hallucinating.

Adam: A whole group of people do not have the same hallucination at the same time. Besides, they were at Jerusalem. They could point to the empty tomb of Jesus. If the religious leaders wanted to prove that Jesus was still dead, all they had to do was to produce His body. But they couldn't do it. Jesus' body was nowhere to be found. He had risen from the dead.

Steve: You mean, you really still believe all this stuff, even after you lost your wife just like I lost mine?

Adam: Yes, I still believe. I'm not saying that this week has been easy for me. I must have asked God a thousand times why He let this happen.

Steve: Did you get any answer?

Adam: Only the answer the Bible gives. Steve, I've been mourning and grieving, too, and it's not over yet. But Jesus knows about that. He cried over the death of a friend of His. And I'm not afraid to admit that I cried myself to sleep last night.

Steve: So did I.

Adam: But in the mourning, I still have hope. Not hope to be with

Cathy again in this world—but hope for the next world. Oh, how I wish you could know that same hope! It's not human hope. It's hope in God. It's what His word says. Jesus said, "Because I live, ye shall live also."

Steve: I don't know. If there is a heaven, and if Carol's there, I want to be there, too.

Adam: I want to be there with Cathy—but more than that, I want to be there with Jesus.

Steve: But like I said before, Carol was such a good person. And I've never been that good. Maybe I'm not a criminal, but I'm no saint like Carol was.

Adam: Steve, Jesus died for your sins, too—all of them. He rose from the dead for you, too, to give you life. He wants to convince you of His promises so that you believe in Him, too. Jesus will keep His promise: "Because I live, ye shall live also."

The End

NOTE: Miss Deana Van Diepen, 16, participated in a youth group production of this play at Mt. Calvary Lutheran Church, Indianola, Iowa, on Easter Sunday, 1989. Driving home afterwards, she was fatally injured in a car accident and died the following evening: Pastor Timothy Scharr used the text and some of the words of the pastor in this play in his funeral sermon, which was very helpful to Deana's family and friends. The funeral director commented that he had never seen a calmer funeral for a young person. The credit for the comfort belongs entirely to Jesus, Who said, "Because I live, ye shall live also."

www.ingramcontent.com/pod-product-compliance
Lightning Source LLC
Chambersburg PA
CBHW050237120526
44590CB00016B/2124